AMERICAN HERITAGE

April 1961 · Volume XII, Number 3

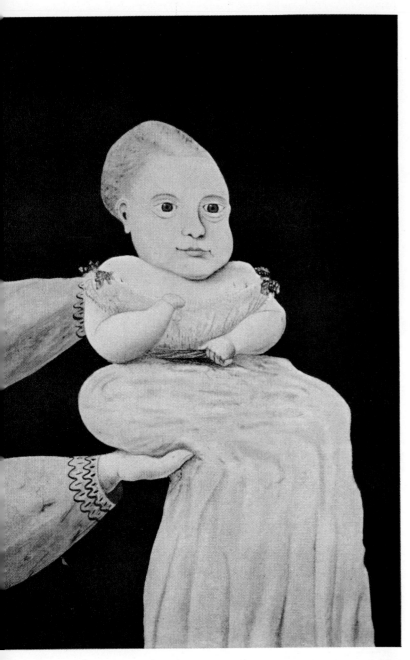

Here, shown in its entirety, is one of the most remarkable nineteenth-century children's portraits
that has come to our attention; it is affectionately
known as Presenting Baby, and is a favorite in the
collection of American primitives at the New York
Historical Association in Cooperstown, New York.
Although the painting has been traced to Rhode
Island, nothing else is known about painter or
subject save that he (or is it she?), no bigger
than a pint of cider and homely as a hedge fence,
nevertheless so appealed to a doting mother
that she had her own arms and hands painted
proudly in. What happened, we wonder, to Baby?

AMERICAN HERITAGE

The Magazine of History

PUBLISHER
James Parton
EDITORIAL DIRECTOR
Joseph J. Thorndike, Jr.
SENIOR EDITOR
Bruce Catton

EDITOR
Oliver Jensen
MANAGING EDITOR
Eric Larrabee
ASSOCIATE EDITORS
Richard M. Ketchum
Joan Paterson Mills
Robert L. Reynolds
ASSISTANT EDITORS
Helen M. Brown, Robert Cowley
Stephen W. Sears
LIBRARIAN
Caroline Backlund
COPY EDITOR
Beverly Hill

SENIOR ART DIRECTOR
Irwin Glusker
ART DIRECTOR
Murray Belsky
STAFF PHOTOGRAPHER: Herbert Loebel

ADVISORY BOARD
Allan Nevins, *Chairman*

Ray A. Billington   Alvin M. Josephy, Jr.
Carl Carmer   Richard P. McCormick
Albert B. Corey   Harry Shaw Newman
Christopher Crittenden   Howard H. Peckham
Marshall B. Davidson   S. K. Stevens
Louis C. Jones   Arthur M. Schlesinger, Sr.

CIRCULATION DIRECTOR
Richard V. Benson

AMERICAN HERITAGE is published every two months by American Heritage Publishing Co., Inc., 551 Fifth Avenue, New York 17, N. Y.
Single Copies: $3.95
Annual Subscriptions: $15.00 in U.S. & Canada
$16.00 elsewhere

An annual Index of AMERICAN HERITAGE is published every February, priced at $1.00. A five-year Cumulative Index of Volumes VI–X is available at $3.00.

AMERICAN HERITAGE will consider but assumes no responsibility for unsolicited material.

Title registered U.S. Patent Office.
Second class postage paid at New York, N. Y.

Sponsored by

American Association for State & Local History · Society of American Historians

CONTENTS   *April 1961 · Volume XII, Number 3*

COVER: A still beardless Abraham Lincoln sat for this brooding charcoal and chalk likeness in Springfield, Illinois, whither a Republican Club of Boston had sent the artist, the now-forgotten Charles A. Barry. Little known for many years, the portrait has recently been part of a traveling exhibition put on by the Addison Gallery of American Art at Phillips Academy, Andover, Massachusetts, and is reproduced here by courtesy of the owner, the Memorial Hall Library, also at Andover. Another kind of portrait of Lincoln, this one in the affectionate words of the telegrapher in whose office the war President spent many anxious hours following the course of events, begins on page 32. Finally, our back cover reproduces six scenes from an old set of magic lantern slides depicting a sad if popular subject in the late 1860's—the murder and death of the President. Though undated, they seem to be nearly contemporary, and come to us from the collection of Messrs. Palmer & Haman, New York.

A century ago this month began the war that set

BROTHER *AGAINST*

ATTACK ON THE MASSACHUSETTS 6ᵗʰ AT BALTIMORE
APRIL 19ᵗʰ 1861.

Sometimes the weariest old clichés turn out to be true. The Civil War was, really, a war of brother against brother. Now and again the brothers come under the magnifying glass and can be seen, hot and bitter against one another.

The Civil War began in mid-April, 1861, with the bombardment of Fort Sumter. President Lincoln called for troops. Among the contingents that headed for Washington was the 6th Massachusetts, which marched through Baltimore on April 19, got into a fight with a street crowd, and reached the capital only after a melee in which both soldiers and civilians were killed.

The riot infuriated many people, among them the Massachusetts-born Pratt brothers. John C. Pratt lived in Boston; his brother, Jabez D. Pratt, lived in Baltimore. Both were sober businessmen, in their forties, and they appraised this fight from opposite angles. When news of it reached Boston, John telegraphed to Jabez, offering him a haven in the Bay State. Jabez replied in anger, blaming all of the trouble on Northern hotheads. Letter followed letter, until at last the brothers were bitter foes, showing—in the words they put on paper—just why the "war between brothers" became a byword. Their letters, furnished us by Mrs. Elizabeth Pratt Holthusen of New York, great-granddaughter of John C. Pratt, are reprinted here as a moving example of the way the war turned good brothers into enraged enemies.—BRUCE CATTON

4

BROTHER

These unpublished letters show how one family was bitterly split

Baltimore, April 20, 1861

My dear Brother:

I have received your dispatch, and while I thank you for your kindness in the offer, we, both Lucy and myself, are not disposed to run,—much less into the arms of infernal abolitionism. We know there is danger. We have expected for thirty-six hours war to the knife. Possibly all may be slaughtered; but by the God in heaven, we are determined to die in the work, and not a man or woman have I seen or heard of but are so determined.

Let any more Northern troops attempt passage of this city and not one will live to tell the story. It is a yawning gulf as long as a man is left to do the death.

Thirty-six hours ago a majority of our people were for peaceable separation, and I may say for peace at all hazards, but now the man does not exist in these parts who is not for the defense of our city against the inroads or passage of troops from the North. We are not to be subjugated by Lincoln and his hordes.

All this has been brought about by the wicked refusal of Lincoln to hear and be advised by Gen. Scott not to send armaments to the South. Gen. Scott begged Lincoln not to do it but he replied, "What in hell will become of the Republican party." [1]

This is the fact and Scott repeated it to Col. Huge of this city who, notwithstanding his being a South Carolina man, has held to the Government till he heard this from Scott and then resigned his commission.

I have just got arms and Joseph and myself intend to do what we can, be it ever so little. If he would not fight I would disown him. But enough.

Your brother
J. D. P.

Boston, Wednesday, April 24, 1861

My dear Brother:

I have just received your letter of the 20th in reply to my dispatch, and I need hardly say that I am pained at its contents. The manner in which you treat my invitation that you would send your wife and little ones to my care where they would be out of danger is cruel and unkind, and I am happy to know several persons who have kindred in your city, and be-

tween whom the kindliest personal relations are kept up and who have received no such response to fraternal offers of protection. The time will come, aye it will sooner than you believe, when you will be proud to proclaim yourself a "son of Massachusetts."

What would you have us do? Would you have us surrender the National Capitol into the hands of that band of mercenary thieves and traitors who rule the "Confederated States"? men who have stolen the public property? who have violated their oaths? Shall we not defend the Capitol? Did not Gov. Hicks say in his proclamation on Friday last that he would furnish troops to do that? And was it not this simple mission and nothing more that our troops were engaged in?

You speak of the South being subjugated by "Lincoln and his hordes." In the first place there is no attempt to subjugate the South, but simply to maintain the Government and that not by "Lincoln and his hordes." No, no. As I told you in my last, the commander of the Massachusetts forces was a delegate to the Charleston convention. Caleb Cushing today offers his services to the Government. Franklin Pierce and every Democrat in the North is willing to bear arms in this contest. [2]

If Baltimore is a "yawning gulf" to bury Northern troops in, the same gulf will bury the last vestige of your beautiful city, for though it cost a hundred thousand lives and "not one stone shall remain upon another" in your city, before this contest ends a *full, safe* and *unobstructed* passage will be opened for our troops to the Capitol.

We do not undervalue Southern prowess; neither can you sneer at Northern courage without proclaiming yourself to be possessed of "Coward's Blood," and let me assure you that you shall have no reason to be

[1] Lieutenant General Winfield Scott, top officer in the Army, never warned Lincoln "not to send armaments to the South," and Jabez Pratt's anecdote is clearly apocryphal. The "Col. Huge" referred to in the following paragraph may have been Major Benjamin Huger, a Regular Army officer who resigned in April, 1861, and became a brigadier general in the Confederate service.

[2] Caleb Cushing was a prominent Boston Democrat who, in the 1860 Democratic convention at Charleston, had stood firmly with the proslavery southern delegates who opposed the nomination of Stephen A. Douglas.

ashamed of Massachusetts troops; as I said at the beginning, you will be proud to say, "I was born in Boston."

J. C. P.

Boston, 27th April, 1861

My dear Brother:

Yours of the 24th with the extract from the Sun is received.

I have read the account of your interview with the President and the result of your mission.[3]

I have no doubt that "Old Abe," as he is familiarly called, is a man of rough exterior, but he is an honest man, and that is better than to have the government in the hands of *polished refined* knaves such as had possession under the last administration, but if he had possessed all the polish and refinement of a "Chesterfield" and had the most fastidious ideas of the dignity of his position, it must have entirely "broken down" before the spectacle of six full-grown boys on such a ridiculous mission.

We read of "the seven wise men of Gotham who went to sea in a bowl." We shall now have the song of the six wise men of Baltimore who went all the way to Washington to ask the President to make an infernal fool of himself, and if his boorishness was equal to your consummate folly and impudence, he would deserve a place in Barnum's museum.

What an astonishing piece of information it must have been to the President to be told by Dr. Fuller and then to be endorsed by yourself that peace would at once be restored if he would recognize the Independence of the Confederate States, give them up all the property they had stolen, and evacuate Washington.

I wonder he had not called his Cabinet together to consult upon the proposition, seize upon it before it "grew cold." I wonder that instead of smiling with ill-concealed contempt he had not grasped your hands and said, "Gentlemen, you have saved the country," and you should each of you have a monument of brass erected to your memory, that being the only material to perpetuate this great event.

Pardon me, my dear brother, if I treat this matter with levity, but I am surprised that you should be a party to this consummate folly.

You may perhaps like to know that Gen. Wigfall has sent his family to Brookline into the arms of "infernal abolitionism."[4]

We are rejoiced to hear as we do this morning that there is a reaction in sentiment in Baltimore and that there is a prospect that our troops will be allowed to pass without a fight. I hope so, for it would be a terrible alternative to be obliged to apply the torch to your city and widen the streets with artillery, for there is no question that if Maryland is obstinate in this matter, she will have to be subjugated. Her secession will amount to nothing: she will not be permitted to go: we like your people too well to part company so easy.

The North is just waking up like the "lion from his lair" as there is a force coming down through the South that will crush out, annihilate, and *sweep away* all before it.

Let the South look out for its cherished institution, let this war continue a few months, and the whirlwind now gathering will sweep within its vortex the South and slavery, and all will perish together. I hope not, but as I have before told you, there is danger.

Love to all.

Yours affectionately
John C. Pratt

Baltimore, April 27, 1861

My dear Brother:

I have just received yours of the 24th.

I wish to say that I fully appreciated your offer of protection made in the kindliest manner and prompted by the kindest personal feeling, and this I said in my former letter. For this I thank you and I know that *you* could harbor no other feelings towards me.

I wish also to say that under similar circumstances I would have done the same for you, and this you well know.

That letter was written under the most intense excitement in this city, and the most of it, so far as it affected me and my friends and the business community, was caused by the deliberate murder (outside of the city after the cars had left for Washington) of my dear friend, Robt. W. Davis, a merchant and one of nature's noblemen. I saw and conversed with him at his store and in the best of humor and spirits. We were starting together to go and see the soldiers pass, without the least idea of any obstruction being offered. I had to go to the office first and we parted, or I should have been with him. He was standing quietly

[3] The reference is to a delegation of Y.M.C.A. leaders from Baltimore, including Jabez Pratt, which called on President Lincoln on April 22 to urge that no more troops be sent through Baltimore; the spokesman for the group, the Reverend Dr. R. Fuller, advised Lincoln to preserve peace by recognizing Confederate independence. Lincoln told the delegates that he had to have troops to defend Washington and that the troops had to cross Maryland to reach Washington, and he added: "Go home and tell your people that if they will not attack us, we will not attack them; but if they do attack us we will return it, and that severely."

[4] John Pratt may be referring to ex-Senator Louis T. Wigfall of Texas, a leader in the secessionist movement, who later became a Confederate general. In his statement that Wigfall had sent his family to Brookline, Massachusetts, Pratt apparently was passing on a groundless rumor.

laughing and talking with two of his and my friends, totally ignorant of any riot or difficulties in the city, and not in any crowd for they had gone away from the city crowd, when a soldier from the platform of the car in very slow motion deliberately aimed and shot him down.[5]

Then it was that the merchants and all the best citizens (not the rowdies) armed themselves to prevent more troops passing via our city, and the tide of popular feeling was aroused and a united determination of resistance went forth.

The city is calm and quiet and order is restored. All the disorder we now have is from the old clubs of "Tigers, Roughs, and Plugs," who are to a man "Black Republicans," and the only ones that we have in Baltimore.

I send you a slip from the "Sun paper," which by the way is a strong Southern paper, which I want you to read.[6] You must permit me to add that while in your house as a guest last summer when the *proprieties* of *hospitality* should have restrained your family even if I had not requested it, I was compelled to listen to sermons on "John Brown raids" which I never can forget, and that is what I called *infernal* abolitionism.

For myself I can hold no other than brotherly affection though we may differ and be separated.

As for being proud of Massachusetts, I long ago lost all such feelings, and if my relations could be moved from the scene I would like nothing better than to see Massachusetts and South Carolina swallow each other up, and I believe it would be a good thing for the world if it could be accomplished.

I understand your eulogies on Massachusetts and do not complain of them, but I do not unite in them. I do not wish to argue the points with you.

We do not want war, much less a war of sections, when neither side can conquer, and when if they could it would be the worst thing which could be done.

We say nothing against the courage of Northern men although it is a notorious fact that the citizens killed were shot by the soldiers while on a run and by turning around and firing to the rear. There are brave men on all sides and it is useless to test the bravery of either.

Now let me say in conclusion that I reciprocate your brotherly feeling towards me, and, if as you intimated in your last letter that if you were called upon you were ready to march, I hope I may not be compelled to meet you in hostility. I would much prefer to meet you as a brother. I don't think you would shoot at the next man to me, and I assure you that such would be my feelings. Of course I mean in my attempt to subjugate the South by the North.

As to defending the Capitol, Lincoln could have got enough men in Washington to have done that, and Virginia would have done it by herself had not the declaration of war been pronounced by him, and this is the same that I told Mr. Lincoln last Monday. But the object is not merely to defend the Capitol.

But enough.

Yours affectionately
J. D. P.

Baltimore, April 29th, 1861

My dear Brother:

I wrote you on Saturday and to relieve anxiety I write again today.

I see the Northern papers filled with inflammable matter and dispatches as to Baltimore which are false. There is no city more peaceable and quiet and not the first particle of "reign of terror." We have in our city Black Republicans and Union men, the latter in large numbers, and who are not fearful in expressing their sentiments, and the B.R. are as safe as in Boston.

There is no muzzling, as in the North. The excitement of our citizens caused by the shooting of our friends has entirely abated. The mob of Friday is deprecated now that reason has its sway. I think the same would have happened in New York or Boston if places and circumstances had been changed to those cities.

Maryland is not going to be hasty and the feeling which before the trouble was prevalent is again shown, that of a peaceable solution of the dispute between North and South.

The whole irritation has been caused by the foolish acts of the administration in declaring war and making enemies of those who were for peace and union for and with the Border States.

We hope for peace and will do all we can for peace.

Yours affectionately
J. D. Pratt

Accept my kind regards and best wishes for yourself

CONTINUED ON PAGE 89

[5] Robert Davis had no part in the Baltimore riot; he seems to have been one of a group of bystanders that set up a cheer for Jefferson Davis as the train bearing the 6th Massachusetts left Baltimore for Washington. His death was a profound shock to the city and undoubtedly made many of its Unionists feel that the Massachusetts soldiers were responsible for the April 19 bloodshed.

[6] This reference is obscure. The Baltimore *Sun* for April 22 carried a statement by Mayor Brown of Baltimore announcing that President Lincoln had asked the Mayor and Governor Hicks of Maryland to come to Washington by special train to confer on "the preservation of the peace of Maryland"; on April 23 the *Sun* announced that a delegation of thirty from the Baltimore Y.M.C.A. had gone to Washington to urge President Lincoln not to send any more troops through Maryland. Whether either of these stories is the one Jabez Pratt refers to here, or whether he enclosed still a different clipping, is not clear.

THE FAMOUS TAX INCLUDED

In one way an Englishman's view of the Revolutionary War does not greatly differ from an American's. Our historians, in the main, agree with yours that the American colonies were lost through the mistakes and obstinacy of George III and Lord North and that the whole episode, whether regarded politically or militarily, is one of the most depressing in British history.

It is at this point that the historians, and even more the ordinary readers, tend to part company. The Englishman, if he overcomes his reluctance to study the period at all, looks at it soberly and objectively and observes how hardly the imperial lesson was learned. Americans, on the other hand, very naturally regard the Revolution with the greatest enthusiasm as the starting point in a series of developments that led to the foundation of a federal republic unique in constitutional history, and to the remarkable political and economic expansion of the nineteenth century. The extraordinary later success of the United States, both in the economic and political sense, has to some extent led Americans to read their history backward and find in the Revolutionary War more signs and portents of a splendid future than were at that time apparent. This provides admirable material for July Fourth oratory, but stretches at places the fabric of history. After all, history is more than an ornamental garden, laid out with hindsight by teachers and historians; it is rather a jungle where living forces were once at work, and the reconstruction of this jungle is our real business if we wish to understand the past.

The first point that I want to suggest is that the conventional picture of the American colonists as a band of gallant pioneers oppressed by a tyrannous government in London is a true one only if looked at through the eyes of a nineteenth or twentieth century democrat. The eighteenth century could have no inkling that the course of history would dictate that colonies in general should become self-administering and finally independent; indeed it was the shock of the American Revolutionary War that first began to teach that lesson. The eighteenth century regarded colonies as existing for the benefit of the mother country, with which, of course, the well-being of the colonies themselves was identified. Adam Smith, no enemy of the colonists, was the classic proponent of this theory. It is sometimes overlooked that the mother country accepted restraints on her own trade or agriculture in the interests of the colony, even if these restraints were of a less onerous character. For example, tobacco growing, although possible, was forbidden in Britain. Foreign produce, which was shipped via Britain, was cheap in the colonies, as duty had been paid by the British taxpayer. Adam Smith commented: "Parliament, in attempting to exercise its supposed right of taxing the Colonies, has never hitherto demanded of them anything which even approached to a just proportion to what was paid by their fellow subjects at home." To this very day, the British subject in the United Kingdom pays taxes at a much higher rate than any resident of the modern British colonies pays to his local administration.

Take next the question of defense. I quote again from Adam Smith: "If any of the provinces of the British Empire cannot be made to contribute towards the support of the whole Empire, it is surely time that Great Britain should free herself from the expense of defending those provinces in time of war . . ." The peace of 1763 had freed the colonists from the fear of attack by the French or Indians, and they naturally felt a greater degree of independence from the mother country. In Britain, however, the legacy of victory was

An Englishman re-examines certain stereotyped attitudes on the American Revolution

By ROBERT CECIL
*Director-General,
British Information Services, New York*

TEA WAS STILL CHEAPER HERE

a burden of debt and a strong feeling of dissatisfaction with the meager contribution, in men and money, that the colonists had made to their own defense. There was angry talk of contraband trade with the French in time of war. A particular grievance was that most colonies were reluctant even to provide adequate quarters for the British troops. This grievance had emerged even before the suspicion that the troops were more likely to be used against the colonists themselves.

When all this has been said, the fact remains that the British government acted with extraordinary stupidity. There was no settled policy of trying either to conciliate the colonists or to exert sufficient force to coerce them while it was still possible. The point I have tried to establish, however, is that the British acted within the framework of the accepted political and economic theory of the day and not out of some feeling of special animosity or desire to oppress the colonists. It is true that "no taxation without representation" was a political principle that many Britons had given their lives to affirm; but here again we are in danger of using hindsight in our interpretation of the word "representation."

England in the eighteenth century was not a democracy; it was an oligarchy, in which no practical politician, however liberal, seriously considered that all men had an equal right to elect the government that ostensibly represented them. A say in the government of the country was the privilege of those whose ownership of property and contribution to its greatness justified their claim.

From this point of view a rotten borough in the hand of a great landowner was a way of ensuring that his contribution to the political and economic life of the nation received its due weight.

In the age of the Whig oligarchy and the rotten borough, there was little to convince Englishmen that the American colonists were being unjustly treated by not being represented at Westminster. It is clear to us today; it was a very debatable point in the eighteenth century. As a matter of fact, the colonists themselves, except the Pennsylvanians, did not take a very liberal view of the franchise for a good many years after the Revolutionary War. The British have never been strong on political theory; they could hardly be expected to realize that across the Atlantic the doctrine of John Locke and the Glorious Revolution of 1688 was believed more literally. Even less could they gaze into the future and divine that the course of the history of the next two centuries would vindicate the judgment of the American colonists. What they saw was a contumacious colony which paid less in taxes than they did, but would neither stand in arms to defend itself, nor pay for the mother country to do so.

Naturally the Americans objected to being taxed; we all do. They fought against the duties levied under the Sugar Act of 1764; the "non-importation" movement boycotted many English goods. The colonists objected even more strongly to an internal (that is, direct) tax, the Stamp Act of 1765, and justification for their position was found on constitutional grounds. The Townshend Acts then, in 1767, imposed a strong external (or indirect) tax, and this was resisted with equal, indeed memorable, vigor. What are we to say of the tea that was hurled into Boston Harbor? The tea had been exempted from the one shilling duty previously payable on transshipment in England and was taxed only threepence in the colonies. The same tea that cost an Englishman six shillings a pound cost the American only three. Yet John Adams wrote of the Boston Tea Party (1773): "Many persons wish that as many dead carcases were floating in the harbour as there are chests of tea." This is not the language of an oppressed people; it is the language of aggressive independence.

The plain fact is that the colonists believed (and events proved them right) that they were fully capable of managing their own affairs; they did not want any control, financial or otherwise. They were equally opposed to any restriction on the way in which they colonized the American continent. They had been made deeply apprehensive by the Royal Proclamation of 1763, which emphasized trade with the Indians and sought to protect them from the territorial encroachment of the whites. But the colonists themselves wished to colonize. Nobody had yet coined the phrase "manifest destiny," but the idea was there. If Britain was opposed, then freedom from Britain must be achieved.

This determination of the colonists to be free was scarcely understood in Britain; indeed their rapidly growing capacity to determine their own fate was lamentably underestimated in London. This explains the failure of the British government either to prepare for war or to make a settlement acceptable to the Americans. For it is probable that up to a very late hour a loose federation with George III as titular sovereign would have been acceptable to the Americans, provided that it carried with it full self-government.

Meanwhile the British made no serious preparation. In 1774, at a time when General Thomas Gage in Boston was asking for twenty thousand men, there were actually reductions both in the Army and Navy. In 1775, General William Howe and his brother Admiral Lord Howe were given the incompatible functions of Commissioners of Conciliation as well as commanders in chief. Inevitably the attack was not vigorously pressed for fear of prejudicing the conciliation; this at a time when George Washington was complaining of the spirit of the men under his command and the totally insufficient arrangements for supplying them. In 1776, Sir Guy Carleton with superior numbers trapped the American forces that had invaded Canada, but deliberately allowed them to escape, believing that a display of magnanimity might show them, as he put it, that "the way to mercy is not yet shut." Though the British were already making use of the Loyalists and the restless frontier Indians, who had long regarded the colonists as their principal enemy, the fighting continued to have some of the characteristics of a civil war; but this first phase was fast coming to an end. By July, 1776, German mercenaries were reaching New York in substantial numbers, and Jefferson, busy with his draft of the Declaration of Independence, referred with horror to their coming.

Meanwhile, in Paris, Silas Deane—and Benjamin Franklin not long after—was negotiating with the old enemy, the Catholic King of France. Lord Stormont, the British ambassador, had a shrewd idea of what was going on, but could not intervene openly. A steady stream of French, German, and Swiss volunteers was crossing in French vessels to the support of the American forces, while French loans and shipments of arms kept the new republic going during the desperate winters of 1776–77 and 1777–78, the winter of Valley Forge. That winter, even after the American forces that had taken part in the defeat of Burgoyne at Saratoga had joined Washington, the General estimated (in December, 1777) that he had only 8,200 fit men under his command. General Howe was unaccustomed, like all who learnt war in the European theater, to campaigning during the winter. He failed to realize that this was the decisive moment—before the French were finally committed to open intervention. Nothing was done and, in effect, the war was lost. It was lost because the limited, colonial war had become a renewal of the worldwide war with France that had merely been suspended in 1763. The French had used the interval to build up their fleet, and they were now able to concentrate it in Atlantic waters. Even before Spain with her Navy joined the Franco-American alliance in 1779, the British had virtually lost command of the sea, and this was bound to prove fatal.

In the first place, it was proving more and more difficult to protect trade and transport men and supplies to the American theater of war. Before the official French intervention took place in 1778, the depredation of American privateers, operating mainly from French ports, had already cost Britain 560 ships and losses equivalent to more than £1,800,000 at rates then current. In 1777, stores that had left England in March did not reach Howe till the end of May, and the summer campaign did not begin till August. Secondly, for their mobility the British forces in America relied to a very great extent on transport by water. Only on rare occasions were they able to operate effectively more than fifteen miles from navigable water. Now all their movements were endangered. In 1778, when Clinton was evacuating Philadelphia, his entire army was almost intercepted at sea by a superior French fleet under D'Estaing. The sealing of Cornwallis' escape routes by the French fleet under De Grasse in 1781 was only the culmination. The capitulation of Yorktown that followed had been written on the wall three years before, for everyone but George III to see.

The retirement of General Howe in 1778 introduced a new handicap. While he was collaborating with his brother, Admiral Howe, relations between Army and Navy had been reasonably good. Afterward, however, old rivalries reasserted themselves. The British Navy was more interested in Rodney's operations in the Caribbean than in transport duty off the American coast. Howe's successor, General Clinton, quarreled with Admiral Marriot Arbuthnot, who had taken up command of the North American station in August, 1778. A British army officer bitterly observed of his brother naval officers: "They do not seem to think that saving the Army is an object of such material consequence." Cornwallis showed an incapacity for combined operations. Significantly enough, he later proved himself a capable general during the land struggle in India.

It is, of course, a truism that generals fight only as well as their opponents permit them to, and we must make every allowance for the genius of Washington, who not only kept his army together in the face of every difficulty but excelled in fighting the defensive war that circumstances imposed on him. He was one of the great leaders of irregular forces. Yet even so, the British generals were strangely inept. A contemporary commented: "This is an unpopular war and men of ability do not choose to risk their reputation." A shrewd contemporary observer regarded Benedict Arnold, in command of British forces, as superior to the *British* generals. The latter had been trained in the European school of set maneuver and siege warfare. Even their rigid discipline put them at the mercy of an irregular force, in which every man was his own company commander, if not his own colonel. The heavy equipment of the regulars immobilized them in the face of lightly equipped forces living off the land —their own land. The American terrain, thickly wooded and crisscrossed with streams and bogs, was unfamiliar to the British, and they failed notably to adapt themselves to it. Washington turned all these failings to good account.

What of the results of this internecine struggle? In the first place, of course, it welded the colonies into a union and equipped them with executive and legislative machinery and the means of defending themselves. This could have been accomplished so rapidly only under the pressure of war. The United States were now free not only to expand their commerce with any part of the world, but to populate the rich lands beyond the Alleghenies. In spite of a generous peace (1783), which astonished the French, relations with Britain did not fulfill the hopes of those in Britain who had always opposed exacerbation of the conflict. The War of 1812 reopened old wounds, and, as the nineteenth century continued, the scars still showed—more clearly perhaps in the United States than in the United Kingdom. I myself believe that some overemotional and unhistorical presentations of the struggle constituted a real hindrance to harmonious Anglo-American relations. It is for consideration whether, even today, a fresh look should not be taken at some of the history textbooks of our two countries.

However that may be, any British view of the Revolutionary War must take into account what future generations of British statesmen learnt from it. Admittedly a generous offer of self-government in 1776, or even early in 1777, might conceivably have brought the war to an end while it could still be regarded as primarily a civil war; but the British did not formulate such an offer until too late. In February, 1778, Lord North was prepared to renounce the right to tax the colonists and to give them virtual autonomy in their own affairs; but by then the Continental Congress was unanimous for independence, and in May, 1778, the treaty with France was ratified. George III had clung too long to the contemporary idea of empire and his own concept of where his royal duty lay. Even a loose commonwealth connection might not have survived the strains and stresses of the Napoleonic Wars and Britain's blockade of Europe.

Leaving the field of speculation, we can be grateful that the American revolutionaries endowed with victory their great federal, republican experiment, without which the world would have been immeasurably poorer. We can rejoice, too, that Britain's failure in her first colonizing venture led thinking men to review the imperial relationship. Can anyone doubt that anything less than defeat could have caused the abandonment of Adam Smith's mercantile system, as applied to colonial territories? And but for this change of heart, the gradual transformation of a colonial empire into a commonwealth of self-governing, independent states could never have been accomplished.

To him, said Morse, art had been only "a cruel jilt." Then
Providence found other work for this complex, difficult Yankee

WHAT SAMUEL WROUGHT

By MARSHALL B. DAVIDSON

*Our inventions are wont to be pretty toys, which distract our attention from serious things. They
are but improved means to an unimproved end, an end which it was already but too easy to
arrive at; as railroads lead to Boston or New York. We are in great haste to construct a magnetic
telegraph from Maine to Texas; but Maine and Texas, it may be, have nothing important to
communicate . . . As if the main object were to talk fast and not to talk sensibly. We are eager
to tunnel under the Atlantic and bring the Old World some weeks nearer to the New; but per-
chance the first news that will leak through into the broad, flapping American ear will be that
the Princess Adelaide has the whooping cough.*
                                                                    —Henry Thoreau, WALDEN

A generation like ours, that feels itself in danger of
being engulfed by the uncontrolled flow of mass
communications, can appreciate Thoreau's forewarn-
ing. But when *Walden* was first published in 1854, the
Western world was celebrating the rapid spread of
electric telegraphy as a consummate triumph of the
human spirit. Those "talking sparks" would cut
through the barriers of space and time and remove
them forever from between the minds of men. Beyond everything the steamboats and railroads could
provide, the telegraph promised a solution to the most
immediate problem of our sprawling American democracy—the union of interests over vast distances.

When the first transatlantic messages were exchanged
a few years later (no references to an ailing princess,
just formal salutations between Queen Victoria and
President Buchanan), devout men talked of the mil-
lennium. Among other widespread demonstrations of
popular excitement, New York was illuminated with
such extravagant zeal that City Hall almost burned
down. The London *Times* re-
ported that "since the discovery
of Columbus, nothing has been
done in any degree comparable
to the vast enlargement which
has been given to the sphere of
human activity." The ocean cable broke several times before
it was finally settled into place
in 1866. But news of that ultimate success came as an anticlimax, at least in America, where
the wonder-working wires had
long since been strung over
longer distances with prodigious
results that were still beyond
calculation.

In December, 1868, a banquet
was held at Delmonico's in New
York to honor Samuel Finley

*The miniature at right is a self-por-
trait of Samuel Finley Breese Morse
in his late teens, painted on ivory
during his student days at Yale.
Morse made pocket money at college
by taking likenesses of his colleagues
and his mentors at one dollar for
a simple profile, five dollars for an
ivory miniature. Left: Morse in his
old age as he was painted in 1900
from memory by his one-time pupil
Daniel Huntington. Morse died in
1872 at the age of eighty-one. When
he was about the age at which he
appears here, a journalist wrote that
"his patriarchal beard—like Mer-
lin's—is his chief sign of age." Huntington placed a palette in his revered master's hand, although Morse
had not touched a brush for years.*

NATIONAL ACADEMY OF DESIGN

13

Breese Morse for his invention of the apparatus that had opened this electrifying new phase in the history of human affairs. He was showered with such eulogies as few living men are privileged to hear spoken for them. Amid a deluge of other tributes, William Cullen Bryant pointed to his aging friend as the man who had taken the most terrible of the elements, "the great electric mass, which in its concentrated form becomes the thunderbolt," tamed it, drawn it through slender wires, and commanded it to serve as an obedient messenger that carried the human language. This was, concluded another distinguished speaker, "the greatest wonder and the greatest benefit of the age." And, as the President of the United States had pointed out to Congress earlier in the year, with these new facilities for intercommunication, the principles of free government could now be broadcast with lightning speed; the messianic role of American democracy would be announced with fresh authority throughout the civilized world.

Morse had become a legend in his own lifetime, his chest a veritable pincushion for medals and awards that had come to him from all over the Western world. It was not then forgotten that, thirty years before, this bearded patriarch had been one of America's leading artists; but it was mentioned with sadness. Daniel Huntington, president of the National Academy of Design, and whilom pupil of Morse, recalled the grief with which he had seen the "beloved master's" sketch remain unfinished on the easel while he strung those mysterious wires around the studio, turning his back forever on the art he had served so well. Huntington never could renounce the hope that his teacher remained at heart an artist. Thus he pictured him, thirty years after his death, in a memorial portrait that showed the aged inventor still clinging to the palette he had put aside so long before. During the intervening years Morse himself had occasionally thought and spoken of returning to his easel. Once he had mastered his "thunder and lightning 'Jim crack,'" he would again pursue the muse and overtake her with the speed of electricity itself. But he never did. With a show of modesty altogether becoming to the great man of the moment, he explained to his banquet audience that he was, after all, but an instrument of Providence. And Providence had dictated that he sacrifice his profession of painting to serve mankind in another way.

In whatever he did Morse was driven by the lofty assurance that he labored in this divinely-ordained service. As a sixth-generation Yankee Puritan, he was acutely aware of his responsibilities to God and man. From the very beginning the sense of personal mission has run in a strong current throughout the course of American history; and it has been inseparable from the larger sense of a national destiny. At both levels that spirit grew more emphatic and more articulate during the first half of the last century, when faith in the American experiment in democracy took on the fervor of a state religion. There was nothing essentially or exclusively Puritanical about it, however. From William Penn and Thomas Jefferson as well, the nation inherited a conviction that in this New World, alone of all places, virtue would be substantially rewarded—that virtue and prosperity would be in fact interdependent. As the country fattened on its natural resources and its ever-expanding economy, it became increasingly difficult to separate the fortuitous and the providential elements in our success and prosperity. Only in very recent years, as our leadership has been challenged and our affluence decried, has there seemed to be reason to make any distinction in the matter.

Out of this fact has stemmed much that is typical and curious about the American experience, from its grand assumption of a Manifest Destiny to the case of Henry Ford, who never was able to separate the Model T from his sense of an individual mission in the

*Shortly before he won parental support of his plans to fol-
low painting as a profession, young Samuel Morse tried out
his budding talent on this conversation piece, representing
the Morse family assembled in the parlor of their Charlestown, Massachusetts, home. The Reverend Jedidiah Morse,
author of the first American geography, stands before a ter-
restrial globe on which all eyes dutifully focus as he explains
some point of learning. The young artist put himself at his
father's left, with his brother Richard alongside. Across
the table are his other brother, Sidney, and his devoted
mother, Elizabeth Ann Breese Morse, her sewing basket
at her feet. Every incidental detail—carpet, Chippendale
chairs and table, and the interior architecture—is picked
out with the conscientious attention of an earnest beginner.*

cause of human welfare. Samuel Morse was a man of
changeable enthusiasms who sought fame and fortune
in several very disparate ways, but his life was unified
by a willingness to fit his own ambitions into the de-
signs of Providence. At times the very stubbornness
of his conviction led him into awkward difficulties and
unworthy contentions; in the end it was the vital
ingredient of his great success.

As a youth, Morse had approached art in a spirit of
consecration. The parsonage at Charlestown,
Massachusetts, where he was born in 1791, was an unlikely background for one who would become a painter.
But the lad had a "calling" that would not be denied.
The urgent nature of that summons was not immediately apparent to his reverend father, Dr. Jedidiah Morse,
who from a distance had observed young Finley at
Yale painting likenesses of schoolmates to pay for the
"seegars" and other frivolities he enjoyed as a student.
But when Washington Allston, brother-in-law of William Ellery Channing and, although a painter, a man
of unquestionably spiritual quality ("one of the pur-
est, noblest, and intellectual beings" Washington Irv-
ing had ever met), endorsed young Finley's aspirations,
Jedidiah unbent. At some sacrifice, and with the pious

hope that their son would "consecrate his acquisitions
to the glory of God and the best good of his fellow
man," the anxious elder Morses sent their son abroad
with Allston to perfect his skill.

They need not have worried. Finley was dedicated
to the noblest ideals of his chosen profession. "My ambition," he wrote home, "is to be among those who
shall reveal the splendor of the fifteenth century; to
rival the genius of a Raphael, a Michelangelo, or a
Titian; my ambition is to be enlisted in the constella-
tion of genius now rising in this country; I wish to
shine, not by a light borrowed from them, but to strive
to shine the brightest." To accomplish this he would
eschew portraiture and landscape and devote himself
to "the intellectual branch of the art," by which he
meant he would be a historical painter. To this end,
in whatever time he could spare from his easel, he
read and studied the works of Spenser, Chaucer, Dante,
Tasso, and others. By historical painting, in turn, he
obviously meant pictures illustrating legends, anec-
dotes, and literary allusions. In March, 1814, he wrote
a friend that he was still hard at his studies. "At present," he continued, "I am preparing a picture for
Somerset House exhibition, 'Dorothea,' from Don
Quixote. I think I shall not be able to see my native
country for some years yet to come; I must return
a painter."

As a token of these high intentions Morse won a
gold medal, oddly enough for his first and only sculpture, a modeled figure of the dying Hercules. Then,
the large painting he had made from the model received extravagant praise when it was hung in the
Royal Academy exhibition. Washington Allston, who
spoke with oracular authority, thought his protégé
would have won further distinction with his next
work, *The Judgment of Jupiter,* but the Morses were
no longer able to support their son in London, and
before the picture could be exhibited Finley had to
return home to make his own living. "If he meets with

TEXT CONTINUED ON PAGE 106
A PORTFOLIO OF ILLUSTRATIONS APPEARS ON THE FOLLOWING PAGES

A QUORUM OF OLD ROMANS

With his Congress Hall, *or* The Old House of Representatives, *a large detail of which is reproduced at the right, Morse hoped to match the success other artists of the time were having in exhibiting historical and religious pictures before crowds of paying spectators. During the fall and winter of 1821–22 he labored up to fourteen hours a day working out the intricate problems of perspective and taking the likenesses of eighty-six individuals, including the Justices of the Supreme Court (standing on the dais at left). His father was in Washington that winter to discuss Indian affairs, and Morse placed him and Benjamin Silliman, along with a Pawnee chief, in the gallery at the right. Morse's primary purpose here, however, was not so much to give highly finished likenesses of these individuals as to present to the public a faithful impression of this celebrated hall during the dramatic moment when the huge brass chandelier with its thirty Argand lamps was being lighted for an evening session. The finished painting, 86½ by 130¾ inches, was convincing proof of Morse's command of his medium. Daniel Huntington later spoke of its "rich, solid, impasted execution, like some great old Venetian painter." Unfortunately, the picture never took with the public.*

Below: A cast of Morse's prize-winning sculpture from his student days in London, depicting the death of Hercules. The artist rediscovered it years later in the basement of the Capitol when he was stringing wires to demonstrate his telegraph before Congress.

YALE UNIVERSITY ART GALLERY

Benjamin Silliman the Elder (1779–1864), first professor of chemistry and natural history at Yale.

GREAT PORTRAITS FROM MORSE'S HAND

Colonel William Drayton (1776–1846)

Although during his formative student years Morse put portraiture, a "trade" he disdained, at the lowest level of the art of painting, he went on to paint a long series of admirable likenesses. His subjects included scores of the nation's most prominent citizens. His first real success came during the winter of 1818 in Charleston, South Carolina, where the best families flocked to his studio to be painted by the visiting Yankee. From this first of several seasons in the South, Morse garnered a purse of more than three thousand dollars. Colonel William Drayton, veteran of the War of 1812, militant southern lawyer, and later a congressman, paid the artist three hundred dollars for his dramatically staged portrait. In 1825 the great Benjamin Silliman and a smoulderingly handsome William Cullen Bryant sat for Morse. Both were his longtime friends, and both were portrayed with sensitive understanding. Silliman, a celebrated professor of science, had taught Morse the elements of electricity during the artist's student days at Yale. Bryant, poet and abolitionist editor of the New York Evening Post, was Morse's most enthusiastic eulogist.

William Cullen Bryant (1794–1878)

An Old Couple, A Coveted Commission

Judge Stephen Mix Mitchell, famed as an impartial Connecticut jurist, member of the Continental Congress and Federalist senator, was a Plutarchian ancient of 84 when painted by Morse in 1827.

The Judge's wife, born Hannah Grant, an heiress from Newtown, Connecticut, bore eleven children. Six sons followed their father to Yale, but the Judge outlived nearly all of them, dying at 92.

In 1825 Morse also painted the most original and impressive of all his portraits, the full-length canvas of Lafayette (right). The picture was commissioned by the Corporation of the City of New York to commemorate the revered General's widely celebrated return visit to America. It was the most coveted commission in America, and Morse was chosen in competition with several of the best-known artists of the day. He placed Lafayette against a glowing sunset to symbolize "the glory of his own evening of life." On his right, an empty pedestal awaits his bust, which would, in time, join those of Washington and Franklin. It was a moment of tragedy as well as triumph for the artist: his beloved first wife died before he could report his elation at meeting the great French hero. Later in life, in Paris, Morse and Lafayette became firm friends.

Shortly after he completed his Lafayette, Morse painted deeply perceptive likenesses of the aged Judge Stephen Mix Mitchell and his wife (above). In his portrayal of those gentle old faces, so strong in character and so rich in composure, Morse demonstrated the full measure of his talent and training. The judge, especially, is one of the finest portraits ever painted in this country.

ART COMMISSION OF THE CITY OF NEW YORK; COURTESY *Time*

In Niagara Falls from Table Rock, *Morse brings the mighty cataract to dramatic, convincing life. Yet the painting in*
other sense only serves to justify further James Fenimore Cooper's rather ambiguous praise of his friend as an ad

ble copyist, who, despite all his aspirations to pursue the "intellectual" in art, painted best what lay before his eyes.
hat seems to have lain before them in this case was an engraving from a much earlier painting by John Vanderlyn.

COPIES & SKETCHES

Morse's notebooks from 1840 to 1842, now kept at the National Academy of Design in New York, are filled with informal sketches, satires, and "studies in physiognomy," most of them unfortunately unidentified or cryptically allusive. He used old magazines for notebooks, as shown below, simply pasting sketches over the type.

On the second of his sojourns abroad, Morse's great project was a large canvas, 76 by 106 inches, showing the famous Salon Carré of the Louvre (above) hung with a purely fanciful arrangement of many of that museum's masterpieces. Among the more noticeable of them are Leonardo's Mona Lisa, Raphael's La Belle Jardinière, Titian's The Entombment, and Van Dyck's Portrait of a Lady and her Daughter. Around the hall, copying busily if less extensively than Morse, are the inevitable students, their teachers, and their admirers. In May, 1832, the painter wrote his brother that his anxiety to finish this one-canvas exhibition was driving him mad. It took him until August, 1833, but when it was shown in New York and New Haven it attracted little popular attention.

25

Morse's Allegorical Landscape Showing New York University, *painted in 1836, is imaginary save for the building at left.*

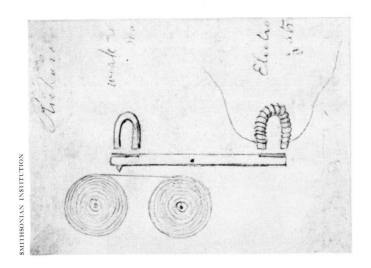

When he painted the Allegorical Landscape, Morse was living and working in the attic of the square tower (above, left) at New York University. So poor that he was bringing in groceries after dark and cooking for himself, he earned small sums by lecturing on art, but spent every available minute on the invention that made many of his friends sadly shake their heads. For here he built his first telegraph, reproduced on the opposite page. As his rough sketch at left shows, Morse was trying to record a signal on a roll of paper passing beneath a stylus set in a lever. The plain magnet at left would hold the stylus up, until a charge passing through the electromagnet at the right pulled the lever up and pressed the stylus against the moving paper.

Morse's first telegraph, below, was mechanically crude, but it contained the germ of a much later improvement—automatic teleprinting. His sending device was a kind of portrule of wood. Through a slot, Morse cranked slugs of metal (A) cut on one side in a sawtooth pattern representing different letters. (These slugs are shown in Morse's own memorandum of the 1837 code, at right, together with some of his later changes.) Passing under the wooden bridge at the center of the portrule, they activated a long arm which made and broke a circuit at the points marked B. Wires led from these points through a battery and connected to an electromagnet (C) at the receiving end. Alternately tugging and releasing a pendulum arm (D) as the power pulsed in the pattern of the message, the magnet caused a pencil (E) to record the original signal on a slowly moving tape. Regulated by an old clockwork (F), the tape was pulled by a weight hung from the pulley (G). Tearing off the completed tape, one now deciphered its short V's, long dashes, and spaces. There was but a single circuit. The use of a key, and a much simpler code to be tapped out with it, came later. The original code was too difficult for an operator to memorize.

While the sending device shown here is a reproduction, the receiver is the original, constructed by the painter out of one of his old frames for stretching canvas. It symbolizes his abandonment of art for invention, and it also symbolizes the seven lean years of beggary and frustration that Morse endured before the government agreed to finance his telegraph. It was in 1844 that the first message went over the wire from Baltimore to Washington.

THE PRIMITIVE
TELEGRAPH

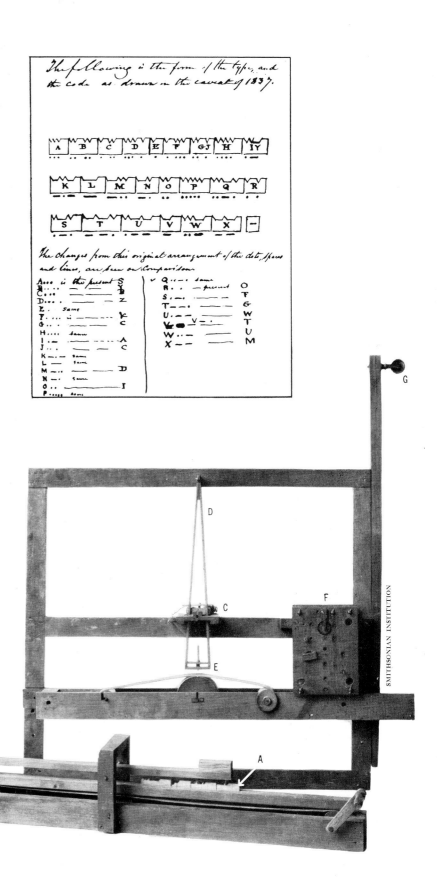

THE TELEGRAPH CROSSES THE SEA

The Atlantic Cable Projectors, *as they were called by the painter of this picture, Daniel Huntington, are shown below at a meeting of that group of inventors and financiers at the Gramercy Park residence of Cyrus W. Field in New York. From left to right are Peter Cooper, David Dudley Field, Chandler White, Marshall O. Roberts, Morse, Huntington, Moses Taylor, Field, and Wilson G. Hunt. A first cable operated briefly in 1858 and broke, and it needed several herculean efforts before the cable was finally and successfully laid in place by the mammoth early steamship* Great Eastern *(right) in 1866 (see "I'll Put a Girdle Round the Earth in Forty Minutes,"* AMERICAN HERITAGE, *October, 1958). More than a half century earlier Morse, as an impatient youthful artist in London, had written his mother that "three thousand miles are not to be passed over in an instant." Now that they might be, he voiced a hope that this new extension of his invention would serve the causes of peace and good will among the peoples of the earth. William Cullen Bryant's imagination went down "to the chambers of the middle sea, to those vast depths where repose the mystic wires on beds of coral. . . . Through those watery solitudes . . . there are gliding to and fro, by night and by day, in light and in darkness, in calm and in tempest, currents of human thought borne by the electric pulse which obeys the bidding of man."*

The steamship Great Eastern *laid the Atlantic cable in 1866.*

Morse's early thoughts on a submarine cable were recorded in this sketch in his notebook of 1842, underneath another of his unidentified portrait sketches.

29

Two Eras, Two Families

Left: According to Daniel Huntington, Morse painted this happy group portrait of his first wife, Lucretia Pickering Walker Morse, and their children, Charles and Susan, as an experiment with colors ground in buttermilk. It is, in fact, unique among Morse's works in its colors and textures, and the artist thought highly of it. When Lucretia died in 1825, while Morse was sketching Lafayette in Washington, he was desolated. "My fear with regard to the measure of my affection toward her was not that I might fail of 'loving her as my own flesh,'" he wrote to a friend, "but that I should put her in the place of Him who has said, 'Thou shalt have no other Gods but me.' I felt this to be my greatest danger, and to be saved from this idolatry was often the subject of my earnest prayers. If I had desired anything in my dear Lucretia different from what she was, it would have been that she had been less lovely."

Years later James Fenimore Cooper jokingly referred to his friend as a confirmed celibate. Nevertheless, in 1848, at the age of fifty-seven, Morse took to wife his deaf, twenty-six-year-old cousin Sarah Griswold, by whom he had four children. In the photograph above, taken about 1860 at his house, Locust Grove, which still stands near Poughkeepsie, New York, are the artist and his wife, seated at center, with two of their children, Cornelia and William, at their right. At their left are Morse's daughter by his first marriage, Susan (whose portrait by her father appeared on our cover of August, 1956), and his second mother-in-law. Morse's son by his first marriage, Finley, stands at the right of Susan's husband, Edward Lind. Morse spent his last years in Poughkeepsie. He encouraged Matthew Vassar to found his college for women and served on the institution's first Board of Trustees. This year Vassar honors him during its centennial year with a Morse exhibit which includes a number of the paintings that are reproduced here.

31

I have always considered that I was fortunate in being one of the three cipher operators in Military Telegraph service in the old War Department building, and to be often with Mr. Lincoln during the time of his greatest burden and anxiety. My immediate associates were Charles Tinker and Homer Bates. Our duties were equal and co-ordinate in the performance of the important and confidential service that we were called upon to render. Mr. Stanton's secretary used to refer to us as the "Sacred Three." Much of the time I alone occupied the room adjoining the private office of the Secretary of War, Mr. Stanton. This was often spoken of as the President's room, for it was to it that he came nearly every day in his anxiety to learn the latest news of the various armies, and the talks he had there with the telegraph boys and Major Eckert, their superintendent, seemed to afford him genuine diversion. Frequently, too, he had interviews there with the Secretary of War, the Secretary of State, and of the Treasury, with the Judge Advocate General, the General in chief, and the other chief officers of the Government.

I first saw Mr. Lincoln at Allegheny, Pennsylvania, when he was on his way to Washington to assume the task of reconciling a great nation to itself. . . . As both telegraph operator and railway agent, I was among the few who were privileged to enter the private car in which he and his family were making their journey, and I shall never forget the deep impression which his towering form and his already sad and always kindly face made on me as he took my hand. . . .

The next time I remember his speaking to me was early one morning, perhaps six o'clock, soon after I went to Washington. I had been on duty all night. He had left the office as late as ten or eleven o'clock the night before, but so anxious was he for news from the armies that he often came over from the White House soon after daylight to see the despatches which had come in during the night. He seemed amused at finding me in exactly the same position, writing at my desk, in which he had seen me the night before, and as he came in he said: "Have you been sitting there all night?" Then he read over the new messages addressed to the various officers of the Government, both civil and military, carbon copies of which we made on letter-size tissue-paper and placed without folding in a little drawer in what we called the cipher desk. The contents of this drawer were for his special information. The messages were placed in it in the order of their reception, and he was careful to keep them so.

It was his habit to read from the top down, and when he came to those which he had already read, with a smile he said: "Well, I guess I have got down to the raisins." As I seemed in doubt as to what that

LINCOLN
and the

TELEGRAPHER

Albert Chandler

Samuel F. B. Morse's telegraph, when the Civil War came, proved to be an essential weapon—permitting the commander in chief personally to direct his armies. No one was more aware of its importance than Abraham Lincoln, who came each morning to the War Department telegraph office across the street from the White House; and few men had a more intimate picture of the wartime President than the telegrapher Albert Chandler, whose recollections appeared forty years later in the now-defunct Sunday Magazine. We are obliged to E. B. Long of Chicago, a Civil War authority, for rediscovering them.

might mean, he explained that a little girl, having eaten improperly both in quantity and quality, beginning with a lot of raisins, was made quite ill, and could find relief only in the process which a sick stomach is likely to compel. After an exhausting siege she gave an exclamation of satisfaction that the end of her trouble was near, for she had "got down to the raisins."

One day soon after this, hearing a newsboy on Pennsylvania Avenue calling out in a singsong way, "Here's yer Philadelphia Inquiry!" he mimicked him, and then said: "Did I ever tell you the joke the Chicago newsboys had on me? A short time before my nomination I was at Chicago attending a lawsuit. A photographer asked me to sit for a picture. This coarse rough hair of mine was in a particularly bad tousle, and the picture presented me in all its fright. After my nomination, this being about the only picture of me there was, copies were struck to show those who had never seen me how I looked. The newsboys carried them around to sell, and had for their cry, 'Here's yer Old Abe! He'll look better when he gets his hair combed,'" and he laughed over it as heartily as if it were a good joke on somebody else. . . .

The President was much in the habit of sitting with his feet on a table, or desk, or chair. In cold weather, during all my observation of him, he wore a large gray shawl, and never an overcoat. This shawl he usually hung over the top of the inner door of the office as he came in, a position in which a man of ordinary height could not place it.

You may like to know, as probably most of you do not, that his composition, in writing, was slow and apparently somewhat labored, and his writing itself was a comparatively slow process. While writing, as I have often seen him, sitting directly opposite me and at the same table, he was accustomed to look out of the window between his sentences, scratch his head, usually his right temple, for his sentences in his mind, often moving his lips in actual whisper of the words, and then write them out, rarely erasing, interlining, or correcting; and when he had finished, what simple and perfect diction it was! His style of composition was as peculiar and novel as himself, and always in simple, terse, and clear language. He sometimes read aloud, and in doing so would occasionally purposely mispronounce words and misplace inflection and accent, as if musing as he read.

His keen sense of the ridiculous extended to little things, and he was as perfect a mimic as his large frame would permit. A good example was this: Albert Johnson, Mr. Stanton's private secretary and personal accountant, was a man of unusually small stature, weighing perhaps a hundred and ten pounds, and his deportment was extremely polite. On one occasion

Mr. Lincoln wanted to refer to the Bible, and he asked Johnson to bring it. Johnson danced out of the room to get it; but not finding it quickly, and fearing that the President might become impatient, he ran back to explain that he had not found it yet, but would have it presently. He finally brought it, with an apology for the delay, and, with low repeated bows, retired. After Mr. Lincoln had made the desired use of the book, he ran nimbly into the adjoining room, just as Johnson had done, reappeared, then made his delivery of the book in the same fashion, greatly to his own and our amusement. This may not strike anybody as funny; but the extreme contrast in the size and movements of the two men, and the close imitation of the mimicry, made it decidedly appear so to us, for whose benefit he performed the bit of acting.

He came to our office, as he said, to "get rid of his persecutors," most of whom wanted to see him "just a minute," which meant that if he could hear their whole case and decide just as they wanted him to do in a minute, then that was all the time they wanted; but that it did not often happen that way.

Peculiar names and alliterations seemed to have a charm for him, and he would repeat them over and over to himself. He was in the habit of talking to himself, as I several times observed when he was walking between the White House and the department.

The Battle of Dranesville was, I believe, the first engagement of the Army of the Potomac under McClellan, and occurred after weeks of spirited picket firing. It, however, accomplished nothing of practical results, and it seemed that both armies were afraid to make a serious attack. After reading the reports, Mr. Lincoln said it reminded him of two puppy dogs he had seen barking furiously at each other through a paling fence. They kept up the most savage snarling as they ran along, until they came to an open gate, when each snapped its jaws at the other, turned quickly around, and ran away. The first news of the battle was to the effect that our forces had whipped the rebels, and among other things had captured fifty Colt's revolvers. Mr. Lincoln read the message aloud, and asked the office messenger who handed it to him if he could tell when those Colt's revolvers would grow to be horse pistols.

One morning after General Grierson's celebrated raid, Mr. Lincoln came in, and as the raid was the most important recent military event, it was made the subject of conversation. Mr. Lincoln remarked that it was a most extraordinary movement. Grierson started into the rebel lines at Memphis, and nothing was heard of him for nearly three weeks, when he arrived safely at Baton Rouge with his command, having done serious damage to the Confederate railroads, machine-shops, mills, etc., along his route. The President said it reminded him of a story he once heard, of a person who had run a needle into his hand and never knew anything of it again till it came out of one of his feet, fifteen years afterward.

When he finished reading the telegrams announcing the result of Sheridan's last fight with Early in the Shenandoah Valley, he said he thought Early's army was in about the same condition as the dog he once heard a man say he had killed. The hateful cur ran fiercely at him, snapping at his heels and annoying him provokingly every time he passed his owner's house, and [the man] determined to be rid of him. So he one day filled a piece of punk with powder, set it on fire as he was about to pass his neighbor's house, clapped it inside a biscuit, and when the dog rushed at him as usual, tossed the biscuit to him. In an instant the dog snapped it up and swallowed it. Presently the fire touched the powder and away went the dog, his head in one place, a leg here and another there, and the different parts of him scattered about; "but, said the man, "as for the dog, as a dog, I was never able to find him." After this last fight, Early's army, as an army, the President said he thought would be hard to find.

On June 14, 1863, information of the extensive movement of the Confederate army toward Maryland and Pennsylvania was received. This proved to be an attempt to transfer the battleground of the war from southern to northern soil, and culminated in the great Battle of Gettysburg. From the beginning of this movement until the recrossing of the Potomac by General Lee, with all that remained of his army, Mr. Lincoln spent much of his life in the War Department telegraph office. During this time General Hooker was relieved from the command of the army, and General Meade was made his successor.

On July 12, upon receiving a message from General Meade explaining somewhat in detail the movements of his army, and of the enemy as far as he could ascertain them, [Mr. Lincoln] called me to a large map hanging near my desk, which he frequently consulted, and pointed out that it seemed to him that the enemy were surely being driven to cross the river, instead of being prevented from doing so. General Meade's message closed with these words: "It is my intention to attack the enemy to-morrow, unless something intervenes to prevent it; for delay will strengthen the enemy and will not increase my force." Calling me again to the map, and pointing out the position of the various portions of the army as he understood them, and reading General Meade's message over again, [Mr. Lincoln] paced the room, wringing his hands and saying: "They will be ready to fight a magnificent battle when there is no enemy there to fight." His apprehensions were proved to be justifiable; for the next morning, when the attack was proposed to be made, the enemy had indeed escaped across the river. . . .

On the seventh of the following August, while I was alone in my office, Mr. Lincoln came in, bringing a long message which he had written with his own hand, addressed to Governor Seymour of New York, who, you may remember, was opposed to the war. He sat down at a desk and carefully reviewed it, so that I might see that it was properly transmitted. He explained to me something of the occasion of it, a special messenger having come over from New York with a long argument urging, among other things, that the draft should be suspended until the Supreme Court had decided as to the constitutionality of the draft law; and he told me a funny story about a Boston minister who had been drafted, and the criticism he made upon that method of recruiting the army.

Perhaps as popular a story as any that have been attributed to Lincoln is that referring to an alleged delegation who appealed to him to remove General Grant from command because of his indulgence of strong drink. The story has it that, after listening to the appeal, the President inquired if any of them could tell him where General Grant got his whisky; "because," he is reported to have said, "if I could find out I would send a barrel of it to each of the other Generals." I heard a gentleman inquire of him soon after this story became current whether it was true. He replied: "That would have been very good if I had said it; but I reckon it was charged to me to give it currency." He said the origin of that story was in King George's time. Bitter complaint had been made to the King that General Wolfe, then operating against Quebec, was mad. "Mad, is he?" said the King. "Then I wish he'd bite some of my other Generals."

I wish to make special and grateful mention of the deep and genuine sympathy which Mr. Lincoln manifested for the soldiers in the field. He did not fail to realize the necessity for the exercise of strict discipline, and yet no soldier boy was ever executed for sleeping on his post or other like offenses, when Lincoln could prevent it. I think I have known him to come over to our offices himself, alone, at least half a dozen times, in the night, with a message of reprieve for some poor fellow who was under the sentence of death which nothing but the President's power could stay, and his solicitude would not allow him to intrust his message to an orderly or other messenger, when a human life depended upon his direct action, and execution might take place unless the official stay was hurried to its destination.

The huge, cloven-footed creature that terrorized southeast Arizona was no figment of the mind. The grisly story of its origin and fate was more macabre in fact than any fiction

THE RED GHOST

By ROBERT FROMAN

One morning in the spring of 1883 two women were alone with their children in a small adobe house on Eagle Creek in the southeastern corner of the Arizona Territory. The men of the family had gone out early to determine how many of their sheep had been slaughtered or driven off by Geronimo and his Apaches in the latest raid through the area. Being left alone at such a time meant a certain danger for the women, since Geronimo might take it into his head to return that way, but to such dangers they had long since been inured.

At some time during the forenoon one of the women left the house to bring water from the spring several yards away in a thicket of willows. A few minutes after she went out, the house dog began to bark and brought the other woman to the window. All she was ever able to report about what she saw was that it was red, enormous, and ridden by a devil.

She heard screams but was too terrified to think of doing anything. Instead, she barricaded the door and spent the day in hysterical prayer. When the men returned that night and heard her story, they lit torches, and went to investigate the spring, where they found the body of the second woman near the water, trampled almost flat. In the mud were the prints of hoofs, cloven and twice the size of a horse's. Clinging to some of the willows were long, red hairs.

The coroner from Solomonsville who held an inquest was highly suspicious of the story. Except for the horribly battered state of the body and the remarkable hoofprints, he would have been convinced

that the woman had been murdered, possibly by other members of the family. In the end, however, he permitted the jury to return a verdict of "death in some manner unknown," and it was so reported in the *Mohave County Miner,* a weekly newspaper in Kingman, Arizona.

A few days later two prospectors washing for gold on Chase's Creek, a tributary of the Rio San Francisco several miles northeast of Eagle Creek, were awakened in the middle of the night when their tent came smashing down on their heads. They heard, as they told it, a loud scream and a sound of pounding hoofs and saw what seemed to them an impossibly tall horse crash off into the brush. When they told their tale at the mining camp of Ore, several miners returned to the scene with them. Along the bed of the creek they found the prints of huge hoofs and through the brush leading off uphill a trail that had been broken by an obviously large animal. A few long red hairs clung to some of the bushes.

Although half a dozen miners corroborated these discoveries, which clearly coincided in details with the occurrence at the sheep ranch, the general reaction to the story was a skeptical grin. Tall tales told around the campfire were the favorite form of entertainment in those days, and the tellers soon seized on the Red Ghost, as they dubbed the mysterious animal, and embroidered on the meager accounts of his two appearances. One devotee of this game claimed that he had chased the beast and that it had eluded him by vanishing into thin air. Another reported that he had watched it kill and devour a grizzly.

The ghost explained: It may have been one of the camels which stood disdainfully by, while horses and men quenched their thirst, in this Narjot painting of the 1857 Army test of camels as desert transportation.

About a month after the death of the ranch woman, however, the Red Ghost rematerialized in a form the tall-tale tellers had not dreamed of. The event took place near the Salt River some eighty miles northwest of Eagle Creek. A rancher named Cyrus Hamblin, out hunting for stray cattle, climbed a bare ridge to get a look around. Across the ravine below him was a tableland covered with dense chaparral. He could barely distinguish a huge reddish animal moving through the brush.

Hamblin later admitted that, despite the deep ravine separating him and this apparition, the hair rose a bit on the back of his neck. But he stayed to get a better look, and the animal gradually worked out into a fairly open space. Hamblin was able to relax. Although the distance was a good quarter of a mile, he recognized the beast beyond any possibility of doubt. It was a camel.

To most Americans, and even to most Arizonans, the discovery of a camel wandering in the wilderness would have been quite as startling as most of the invented stories about the Red Ghost. It happened that Hamblin had spent several years in the desert region of the southwestern part of the territory near the California border. He had never heard of camels in the high Salt River country, but he knew that in the desert they were, if not plentiful, by no means uncommon. He also could see that there was something more

unusual about this camel than his choice of range. The hump on his back was topped by an oddly shaped burden. At the distance separating them, Hamblin was unable to see the burden clearly, but he reported that it looked to him like a man. And if it was a man, it seemed quite certain that he was not alive.

Hamblin's reputation was so solid and his story so soberly circumstantial that most of it was widely accepted. It brought back to life a nearly forgotten bit of the West's history and gave the more imaginative of the territory's citizens something they could really go to work on. Soon the Red Ghost, or *Fantasia Colorado* as the Spanish-speaking settlers called it, was one of Arizona's most famous inhabitants.

The one suspect item in Hamblin's account was the matter of the burden on the beast's back. Scoffers were convinced that it was merely the camel's hump. But a few weeks after Hamblin's experience, the Red Ghost turned up near the valley of the Verde River about sixty miles west of Hamblin's ranch, and the scoffing ceased. This time a party of five prospectors sighted the animal feeding on a mesa, managed to get within what they considered shooting distance, and banged away. They either missed completely or merely grazed the animal, and it rapidly loped off out of range. As it departed, something fell from its back. The prospectors investigated and found, as the *Mohave County*

36

Not banshees but Bactrians: *During a halt in the High Sierra, a camel majestically surveys the scene, a wagon train appearing in the distance. The sketch,* Descent to Carson Valley, *was made by Edward Vischer.*

Miner described it, "a human skull with a few shreds of flesh and hair still clinging to it."

This gruesome discovery firmly established the Red Ghost as a living legend. Its career in that role was to last nearly ten years. Since the only contemporary account of this career seems to be the one in the *Miner,* and since newspapers in those days were by no means slaves to facts, it may be that some of the details were improvised. Most of them were reported so circumstantially, however, that this is unlikely, and none was the kind of obviously farfetched fiction the more imaginative western editors commonly went in for. The latter also were not up to inventing the ferocious human malevolence toward animals involved in the story of the Red Ghost.

The Ghost's career made a fitting conclusion to the pathetic history of the U.S. Army's First (and only) Camel Corps. That history had begun hopefully enough, if rather belatedly, in March, 1855, when President Franklin Pierce's Secretary of War, Jefferson Davis, persuaded Congress to appropriate thirty thousand dollars for the purchase of camels to be used by the Army in exploring the Southwest. Like most military innovations, this one had been proposed many years earlier. One of the explorers of the West, Major George H. Crosman, had formally recommended in 1836 that, since the chief desert problem was lack of water and since camels could go longer without it than horses or mules, the Army should experiment with the use of camels. It took the suggestion nineteen years to work its way up through channels.

When Davis finally got the money for the project, he sent Major Henry C. Wayne and Lieutenant David D. Porter to the eastern Mediterranean in a Navy storeship, the *Supply,* to buy the first camels. An experienced horse trader, Wayne took plenty of time investigating camel lore and studying the offerings in the camel markets of Alexandria and Smyrna. It was time well spent. All but one of the thirty-three animals he bought at an average of $250 apiece survived the tough, three-month voyage to Indianola, Texas, and two colts (camel young were so called in the King James version of the Bible, and the Americans adopted the term) were born on the trip.

Wayne and Porter also hired six Arabs and a Turk, the former as camel drivers and tutors to the Army's muleteers, and the latter as a veterinary. Their remarkably bad judgment in these hirings foreshadowed the ultimate fate of the experiment. Apparently they assumed that since camels abounded in the Levant, any Levantine must be a camel expert. The Arabs were about as familiar with camels as the average city boy today is with horses, and the Turkish veterinary's treatment for a sick camel, whatever the ailment, consisted of tickling the animal's nose with the tail of a chameleon.

CONTINUED ON PAGE 94

A FACE FROM THE PAST—I

He is the President no one knows. If school children remember him at all, it is as a name that comes somewhere between the Mexican War and the Civil War—and that judgment is strangely close to the heart of the matter. The generation of Webster, Calhoun, and Clay was gone by 1852. In Baltimore, where the divided Democrats were meeting to select a presidential candidate, forty-eight ballots failed to produce a two-thirds vote for any of the contenders. Then, on the forty-ninth, the delegates gave the nomination to Franklin Pierce of New Hampshire, whose only virtue seemed to be that no one hated him enough to keep it from him. He was safe, and safe was what a man had to be in Baltimore in 1852.

On the advice of older, wiser politicians, the candidate did as little as possible and said almost nothing during his campaign against General Winfield Scott. The Whigs called him coward, a drunkard, and an anti-Catholic, and there was some substance behind each ugly charge; but when the ballots were counted, Franklin Pierce had 214,000 more than Scott, 254 electoral votes against 42, and that was all that mattered—or so it seemed.

His program, he said, would be to provide territorial and commercial expansion (which would please the radicals) and to preserve the Union (which would keep the conservatives happy). Pierce considered it a safe, sound policy, and if the year had not been 1853 it might have been. But just then it was perhaps the most difficult and dangerous course he could have steered.

In an effort to achieve harmony, he gave representation in his cabinet to every faction in the Democratic party, thereby ensuring trouble under the best of circumstances. Only there were to be no best of circumstances, but instead a violent eruption of national emotions. The Administration's Kansas-Nebraska Bill resulted in Bloody Kansas; the anti-foreign, anti-Catholic movement took dark shape in the Know-Nothings; westward expansion and industrialization were shaking the uneasy balance which had existed between North and South, and southerners saw the handwriting on the wall. The times demanded daring and ingenuity and brilliance, but Pierce had none of them; nor did he comprehend the irresistible tide of forces he was attempting to stem. So at the end of four years, with the nation rushing toward disaster, the Democrats took the unparalleled course of turning their own man out and selecting another who appeared to be safer even than Pierce had seemed in 1852—James Buchanan. And Franklin Pierce, fourteenth President of the United States, disappeared from the stage of history as ignominiously as he had entered upon it.

But there is more to his story than posterity has cared to remember, and much of it is revealed in the photograph Mathew Brady took at the time of his inauguration. This is not the proud, determined look of an incoming President; it is the haunted expression of a man drained of vitality, unaware of the camera, whose deeply troubled eyes search the distance as if seeking some answer to his questions.

The first years of his life had been good ones, and Franklin Pierce emerged from New Hampshire politics to become a United States congressman and senator. Then fortune turned against him. His first son lived only three days; his second died at the age of four. His wife, a melancholy, deeply religious invalid, hated Washington, partly because of the climate, mostly because of the alcoholic temptations to which politics subjected her weak husband. Against her wishes he had gone to Mexico as a political general, and there fate gave him three opportunities for glory. The first time in action his horse shied, the pommel hit Pierce in the groin, and he fainted; the next day, advancing with his troops, he twisted a knee and fainted again; and at the storming of Chapultepec, where he had his last chance, he was in bed with diarrhea.

Five years later fortune beckoned once more, this time with the incredible offer of the nation's highest office, which Pierce saw largely as an opportunity to build a heritage for eleven-year-old Bennie, his surviving son. (When he heard the news of his father's nomination, Bennie wrote his mother: "I hope he won't be elected for I should not like to be at Washington and I know you would not either.")

Early in January, 1853, two months before the inauguration, the Pierces were riding the morning train to Concord. A mile out of Boston it was suddenly derailed; their car teetered over an embankment and rolled into the field below. Neither the President-elect nor his wife was injured, but Bennie, the one absorbing interest of their lives, was caught in the wreckage and horribly killed before their eyes.

From that moment on the prospect of the Presidency became a nightmare. From the twisted depths of her Calvinistic conscience, Mrs. Pierce fashioned the idea that her husband's great honor had been purchased by the sacrifice of their son. With this shattering accusation of guilt added to the unimaginable horror of the boy's death, Franklin Pierce went to Washington, alone, to lead the United States in its hour of need.

—*Richard M. Ketchum*

The poster at left celebrates the Red Army successes against its White Russian foes in 1919. Above, a Communist broadside of 1920 depicts the workers of the world overthrowing their capitalist oppressors.

Ideologies opposed: peasant fights Czar, Church, and Capitalism (top); and a German anti-Bolshevik poster.

AMERICA AND RUSSIA: PART VIII

THE WASTED MISSION

Against a background of postwar turmoil, a 28-year-old State Department aide was sent to negotiate with the Bolshevik leaders. His rebuff by Wilson caused a national uproar

By ROBERT S. RIFKIND

The youthful son of a wealthy Philadelphia family, William C. Bullitt had but recently entered diplomatic service when he headed our first mission to post-revolutionary Moscow.

Russian Communists and their Ukrainian allies are exhorted to overthrow Polish landowners.

Czarist poster (top), and Communist attack (below) on national boundaries.

The stately Hotel Crillon on the Place de la Concorde was a scene of frenzied activity in the early months of 1919. It was filled with 1,300 Americans who had come to Paris for the peace conference that would end the First World War. The corridors swarmed with ethnologists, geographers, economists, interpreters, army officers, reporters, and ambassadors. On occasion, President Wilson, the first American President to cross the Atlantic while in office, could be seen hurrying to keep an appointment with his top advisers.

Out of this confusion was to emerge the first postwar American effort to make contact with Soviet Russia—a mission that matched in its extemporized haste the ignorance and vagueness of United States policy toward the Bolsheviks (*see* "When the Red Storm Broke," AMERICAN HERITAGE, February, 1961). At its head would be placed a young and little-known State Department aide, long on enthusiasm but short on experience, to whose intense dismay this attempt at communicating with the emergent Communist colossus was to end in misunderstanding, bitterness, and ruptured diplomatic relations. His name was William C. Bullitt—the same man, ironically enough, who was fourteen years later to pick up the threads where they

had been broken, and return to Moscow as our first ambassador to the Communist regime.

The excitement and haste that prevailed in the Hotel Crillon—and elsewhere in Paris as well in 1919—was understandable: the world was being made over. New countries were being created and old empires dissolved. A society of nations was being founded. Colonies were changing hands. Boundaries were being redrawn. "The history of the world," President Wilson told the opening session of the peace conference, ". . . will now be crowned by the achievements of this Conference." The lights burned late at the Crillon.

Elsewhere in Europe all was turmoil. After four years of total war the nations of the continent were in a state of political collapse, and no one could tell with certainty what new structures would emerge from the rubble. A major source of uncertainty was the year-old Soviet regime in Moscow—the regime that had made a separate peace with imperial Germany and that was, therefore, not invited to the peace conference. This abrasive newcomer to the world scene was throwing off sparks which, many thought, were likely to ignite Europe. In January, 1919, there was a Communist-inspired revolt in Germany. And in March a successful revolution placed the Russian-trained Béla

41

Lincoln Steffens

Kun at the head of a Hungarian Soviet. "Paris cannot be understood without Moscow," the chief of the press bureau of the American commission later wrote. "Without ever being represented at Paris at all, the Bolsheviki and Bolshevism were powerful elements at every turn. Russia played a more vital part at Paris than Prussia! For the Prussian idea had been utterly defeated while the Russian idea was still rising in power."

Sailing to France on the U.S.S. *George Washington* on December 4, 1918, Wilson had outlined the task facing the American Commission to Negotiate the Peace. As recorded by one of his auditors, Wilson said, "The *poison of Bolshevism* was *accepted readily* by the world because '*it is a protest against the way* in which *the world has worked.*' It was to be our business at the Peace Conference to fight for a new order. . . ." But the Red serpent had already entered Wilson's Garden of Eden. In building a new order, what was to be done with it? Welcome it? Tame it? Crush it? One thing was certain: one could not safely ignore it.

On Sunday afternoon, January 12, 1919, the Council of Ten which was to guide the peace conference gathered for the first time in the ornate office of French Foreign Minister Stéphen Pichon at the Quai d'Orsay. The Russian problem was raised at once. Though the guns were now silent on the Marne, war was in progress between the Soviet regime in Moscow and the White armies based in Siberia, at Archangel and Murmansk, in the Don region and the Ukraine. It would be absurd, the British Prime Minister, David Lloyd George, pointed out, for the Allies to "separate and announce that they had made perpetual peace when Siberia, which formed about half Asia, and Russia, which formed about half Europe, were still at war."

Even if they had wanted to, the Allies could not ignore the Russian situation, because thousands of Allied soldiers had been sent in prior to the German armistice, in the hope of averting a total collapse of the eastern front. (*See* "Where Ignorant Armies Clashed by Night," AMERICAN HERITAGE, December, 1958.) These soldiers soon found themselves buttressing the White armies. Unless there was a cease-fire in Russia they could not be readily extricated.

In the United States and Britain the popular demand to bring the boys home was growing in volume and could not be ignored. Yet a British proposal that the Whites and Reds be invited to suspend hostilities in Russia and send representatives to Paris was widely denounced. "The French Government," M. Pichon announced to the press, ". . . will make no contract with crime." And Joseph Tumulty, Wilson's press secretary, wired from the United States that the suggestion that "the Russian Bolshevik be invited to send peace delegates to Paris . . . is denounced here as amazing." The French could not forget that the Soviets had made a separate peace with Germany, deserting France in the hour of her peril. And America, however eager to get the boys home, didn't care to talk about it with the perpetrators of the Red Terror who had, it was said, nationalized women!

Lloyd George explained that he was not proposing that the Red and White regimes be given official recognition, but rather that they be summoned to Paris "somewhat in the way that the Roman Empire summoned chiefs of outlying tributary states to render an account of their actions." The French remained obdurate; they would listen to representatives of the White regimes who were already in Paris, but not to any Bolshevik representatives. Wilson supported Lloyd George. The White governments, led as they were by former czarist officers, represented the *ancien régime.* Moreover, Wilson said, "there was certainly a latent force behind Bolshevism which attracted as much sympathy as its more brutal aspects caused general disgust." Since further Allied military intervention in Russia was impractical, the Reds and Whites must be encouraged to reach a settlement.

The French were unmoved. In order to meet their objections, Wilson on January 21 proposed that the various Russian factions be asked to send representatives, not to Paris, but to some more remote place where the danger of Bolshevik contagion would be less. Since the Bolsheviks were representing the Allies as supporters of reaction, Wilson argued, the Allies should "show that they are ready to hear the representatives of any organized group in Russia, provided they are willing and ready to come to one place, to put all their cards on the table, and see if they could not come to an understanding."

The French premier, Clemenceau, was still opposed to conversations with the Bolsheviks "in principle" because "we would be raising them to our level by saying that they were worthy of entering into conversation with us." He reluctantly agreed to Wilson's proposal, however, and the following day a proclamation was sent out from Paris inviting the parties involved to a meeting on Prinkipo Island in the Turkish Sea of Marmara not later than February 15. The French, though they had capitulated at the conference table, had not given up; their Foreign Office promptly advised the White governments to reject the invitation. The Unified Governments of Siberia, Archangel, and Southern Russia soon announced that "an exchange of ideas . . . with the participation of the Bolsheviks" was out of the question.

In this state of affairs, the Russian question was reviewed by the Council of Ten on February 14. Wilson was leaving Paris that very night for Washington, to argue for the League. Winston Churchill, who was sitting in for Lloyd George, pressed vigorously for large-scale armed intervention. (The Prime Minister was in total disagreement with his somewhat irrepressible junior.) Wilson rejected intervention as worthless. "What the Allies had in mind," he said, "was the establishment of peace in Russia as an element of the world's peace." In view of the collapse of the Prinkipo proposal, Wilson declared that he would be content "that informal American representatives should meet representatives of the Bolsheviks." What was wanted "was not a *rapprochement* with the Bolsheviks, but clear information." Precisely what Wilson had in mind never became entirely clear. Immediately after his conversation with Churchill on February 14, he departed from Paris, leaving Colonel Edward M. House in command of the American peace commission.

Reports from an American agent in Stockholm had indicated that the Soviets were eager for conciliation and purported to be well disposed toward the proposed League of Nations. Reports from the Villa Majestic in Paris, where the British peace commission was encamped, indicated that the British were "prepared to meet at Prinkipo, or anywhere else, the Soviet Government's representatives, even if no other Russian representatives should accept the recent Peace Conference invitation." In the light of these developments, Colonel House acted swiftly. Within twenty-four hours after Wilson's departure, he was discussing with Secretary of State Robert Lansing the possibility of sending William Bullitt, one of the younger members of the American peace commission, to Moscow.

During the next few days House and Bullitt discussed the peace terms which would be acceptable to the United States. House indicated that the armistice on all Russian fronts, the withdrawal of Allied troops, and the re-establishment of economic relations would form an acceptable basis for a Russian settlement. Bullitt also called upon Philip Kerr, Lloyd George's private secretary (later to become Lord Lothian, British Ambassador to the United States). In Kerr's opinion it was possible to resume normal relations with Soviet Russia on substantially the same terms as House had proposed.

In view of the hostility of the press and the French toward anything that suggested possible recognition of the Soviet regime, it was decided that Bullitt's mission should be kept confidential. On February 18, his credentials were signed by the Secretary of State: they directed him to "proceed to Russia for the purpose of studying conditions, political and economic, therein, for the benefit of the American commissioners plenipotentiary to negotiate peace. . . ." Bullitt was to be accompanied by his secretary, R. E. Lynch, and by W. W. Pettit, a captain in American Military Intelligence traveling in mufti.

At the last minute Bullitt asked Lincoln Steffens to join his party. Steffens was an outspoken admirer of the Soviets and readily agreed to go. In 1919 the once popular muckraking journalist was considered a dangerous man. No major American newspaper or magazine would carry his work, and he was "covering" the peace conference on his own.

On February 22 Bullitt's party left Paris for London. That evening Steffens wrote a friend: ". . . I am here only in transit: going somewhere else. I can't say where . . . I feel as if I were going to see a good play at a good theater." The next day a British naval vessel was to carry them across the North Sea. They would proceed across Scandinavia and enter Russia via Finland. It was a long, cold route to Russia, but in the winter of 1919 it was the only route; America was officially still at war with central Europe.

It was a strange affair, America's first diplomatic

Bullitt (front row, center) posed with members of the American Peace Commission at Versailles. Also in the front row were two others who would become well-known; Christian A. Herter (second from left) and Allen W. Dulles (far right).

mission to Soviet Russia, dispatched with much haste and little thought. When it was over, no one except Bullitt would be quite sure why it had been sent. Bullitt later said:

I was instructed to go in and bring back as quickly as possible a definite statement of exactly the terms the Soviet Government was ready to accept. The idea in the minds of the British and the American delegation were [sic] that if the Allies made another proposal it should be a proposal which we would know in advance would be accepted, so that there would be no chance of another Prinkipos proposal miscarrying.

But Bullitt's credentials merely said that he was to study "conditions, political and economic." Nor was it entirely clear whether Colonel House and Philip Kerr had spoken with authority in formulating the American and British terms with which Bullitt had been furnished.

The personnel of the mission also presented a somewhat odd picture. Bullitt himself was twenty-eight years old. Years later Janet Flanner—"Genêt" of the *New Yorker*—was to describe him thus: "Headstrong, spoiled, spectacular, something of a nabob, and a good showman, he has complicated ambitions which are a compound of his devotion to his own notions of idealism, his interest in his career, and his faith in the ultimate fate of the human race."

The son of a wealthy Philadelphia family, he had traveled much, been graduated from Yale, and spent a year at the Harvard Law School. With the outbreak of war in Europe (he was traveling in czarist Russia at the time), he became a reporter for the Philadelphia *Public Ledger;* when the United States entered the war he joined the State Department to prepare reports on developments within the Central Powers. His job in Paris had been to brief each of the American commissioners, including the President, for twenty minutes each morning on current affairs. (When Bullitt couldn't make the rounds, the future Secretary of State, Christian Herter, was his understudy.) Colonel House knew Bullitt to be keenly interested in the Russian revolution and international socialism in general.

Thinking back on the trip to Russia years later, Lincoln Steffens recalled that "Bullitt had brought along his secretary Lynch, apparently to play with. On trains and boats they skylarked, wrestling and tumbling like a couple of bear cubs all along the Arctic Circle. A pretty noisy secret mission we were, but Bullitt knew just what he was about; nobody could suspect us of secrecy or importance; and at formal moments and in emergencies the head of our mission was all there with the form, the authority, and the—audacity."

On the evening of March 8, the party arrived in Petrograd. The Soviet officials who met the Americans were at first under the impression that the older and more famous Steffens was the head of the mission. They were soon disabused. Indeed, there was some uncertainty as to whether they should deal with the mission at all. Soviet Foreign Minister Grigori Chicherin decided, however, that Bullitt was worthy of being brought to Moscow to see Lenin.

Bullitt and Steffens, together with Chicherin and Maxim Litvinov, arrived in Moscow on March 11. It was a cold and hungry city. For the next few days Bullitt and Steffens lived largely on the canned goods they had brought with them in mail pouches—supplemented by black bread and caviar which alone seemed to be in plentiful domestic supply. Even so, Russian officials had a way of coming by their rooms at meal times.

"When I called on Lenin at the Kremlin," Bullitt later reported, "I had to wait a few minutes until a delegation of peasants left his room. They had heard in their village that Comrade Lenin was hungry. And they had come hundreds of miles carrying 800 poods [or, incredibly enough, 14½ tons—*Ed.*] of bread as the gift of the village to Lenin. . . . Lenin is the only leader who receives such gifts. And he turns them into the common fund."

"Face to face," Bullitt noted, "Lenin is a very striking man—straightforward and direct, but also genial and with a large humor and serenity." He also noted that "the hold which Lenin has gained on the imagination of the Russian people makes his position almost that of a dictator."

After four days of negotiations in Moscow, Bullitt was given a statement of terms which the Soviet government would accept as the basis for a conference if they were proposed by the Allies before April 10. The terms were essentially the same as those suggested by House and Kerr. The most striking element in the proposal was that the Soviet government purported to be willing to leave the White governments in control of the territory they then occupied. This meant that the Bolsheviks would give up (at least for the time being) claim to the whole of Siberia, the Urals, the Caucasus, the Archangel and Murmansk areas, Finland, the Baltic states, a portion of White Russia, and most of the Ukraine. Soviet Russia was to be limited to a radius of some five hundred miles around Moscow.

Satisfied that he had gotten what he had been sent to get, Bullitt left Russia in a rush. From Helsinki he cabled a preliminary report to Paris. On receiving it, House expressed eagerness that the proposals be put in writing (which they were) and wished to wire congratulations to Bullitt. Lansing and others were dubious. One of the proposed terms was that Russians have full right of entry into other countries; some feared this was an invitation to propaganda and subversion.

Bullitt himself got back to Paris on March 25, and that evening he went to see House. Both men knew that it would take a struggle to put over what amounted to a *de facto* recognition of Soviet Russia, but both seem to have thought that it was the only intelligent course. Bullitt filed a final report which was sent on to Wilson. The Soviet regime, it said, had come to stay; and the peace conference should make proposals similar to the ones which the Soviet government had indicated it was ready to accept. Steffens submitted a report to much the same effect. He made it clear that, in his view, the revolution in Russia was over. "The present Russian Government," Steffens wrote, "is the most autocratic government I have ever seen." In a world that still tended to equate Bolshevism with anarchy and instability, Bullitt and Steffens were providing needed information.

The day following Bullitt's return, he and House set out to put over the plan. Bullitt conferred at length with the American peace commissioners. House attempted to deal with the President, who had by this time returned to Paris. But Wilson did not wish to take up the Russian question at the moment. He had, he said, a "one track mind," and it was preoccupied with other matters. The Council of Four was now meeting daily in secret sessions; a crisis over the terms of the treaty with Germany was rapidly approaching. To make things worse, Wilson was at this time increasingly unwell.

Unable to get an appointment for Bullitt with Wilson, House made arrangements for him to meet with Lloyd George and other British statesmen. Bullitt had breakfast with the Prime Minister on March 27. To Bullitt, he seemed greatly impressed with the necessity of making peace with the Soviet government, but worried about public opinion in England. An editorial in the London *Daily Mail* had attacked any attempt to accredit "an evil thing known as Bolshevism." Lloyd George showed the editorial to Bullitt and asked: "As long as the British press is doing this kind of thing how can you expect me to be sensible about Russia?" Questioned in the House of Commons some three weeks later about rumors that diplomatic approaches had been made to the Soviets, Lloyd George replied: "We have had no approaches at all . . . I think I know what my right honorable friend refers to. There was some suggestion that a young American had come back from Russia with a communication. It is not for me to judge the value of this

CONTINUED ON PAGE 72

Ambassador's Return: 1933

On the evening of December 8, 1933, William C. Bullitt boarded a train bound from Paris to Moscow. This time he traveled as the first American Ambassador to Russia since the Bolsheviks had come to power in 1917. For Bullitt, who had long worked for the recognition of the Communist government by the United States, it seemed a moment of triumph. As one observer commented, his new appointment was a chance for him to "enjoy from a box seat one of the greatest mass social experiments in history . . ."

Though Bullitt had all but retired from the public scene after his sensational testimony before the Senate Foreign Relations Committee in 1919, the intervening years had not been inactive ones. He had lived in the Bosporus and consulted with Freud in Vienna, raised German shepherds and McIntosh apples in New England, and had written a best-selling novel, *It's Not Done.* For a brief time he had been married to Louise Bryant, widow of the American Communist John Reed, whose ashes are enshrined in the walls of the Kremlin (*see* "The Harvard Man in the Kremlin Wall," AMERICAN HERITAGE, February, 1960).

As ambassador, Bullitt worked with his accustomed zeal, making heroic efforts to cement the long-lost friendship of America and Russia (he even brought with him quantities of baseballs, bats, and gloves). But he came to realize that the idealistic social experiment of 1917 had hardened into an oppressive dictatorship. Later, after World War II, he was to become an outspoken critic of the "soft" policy toward the Soviet Union. In 1936, however, more in sorrow than in anger, a disillusioned Bullitt left his Russian post to become ambassador to France.

Newburyport, Massachusetts—the modest seaport town at the mouth of the Merrimack River—is immoderately rich in social history. Under the name of "Yankee City," Newburyport has been the subject of an intensive sociological study by W. Lloyd Warner and his associates, published in five volumes which picture the subtle division of its inhabitants into grades of class and status. The son of an old Newburyport family, John P. Marquand, remained until his death last July the nation's most effective novelist of manners and customs, of social aspiration and decline. And Newburyport, too, was once the home of an extraordinary individual named "Lord" Timothy Dexter, in whom sudden wealth and prominence worked to produce an exceptional extravagance of character—a man Mr. Marquand has described as "one of the greatest eccentrics so far produced in America."

Dexter is fascinating in himself, but he was particularly fascinating to John P. Marquand. Lord Timothy was the subject of his two only works of non-fiction, one of them published in 1925, before *The Late George Apley* had established Marquand's reputation as a novelist, the second in 1960, the very last volume he wrote. Marquand returned to Dexter out of dissatisfaction with his first effort—"it embarrasses me to pick it up again"—and out of a concern for achieving balanced historical judgment. In many ways, no one could be better qualified for the task than a novelist like Marquand, in whose pages his own times live with an accuracy and understanding which future historians well may envy. Yet increasingly he had come to realize how remote was the Newburyport of today from the town he had grown up in, and how infinitely more remote, therefore, we now are from the Newburyport of Dexter's day. His last book was an effort to feel his way back through his own past to the past of Revolutionary America. It is a meditation on the impossibility of ever knowing exactly how history felt to those who lived it, and in the process of writing about him Dexter became, for the author, something far more than a famous eccentric.

Eccentric he no doubt was. Newburyport's first real family fortunes, like those of the Tracys and the Jacksons, were made through privateering in the early days of the Revolution. Timothy Dexter, a leather-worker of small wealth and low status, rose with the town's general prosperity, and foresightedly invested his gains in government securities then selling for below their face value. Later, when Alexander Hamilton reformed the monetary system and refunded the foreign and domestic national debt at par, Dexter overnight became a man of substance. Always an individualist, and temperamentally unprepared for the high station in which he found himself, he now became a local character. He addressed vigorous, ill-spelt letters to the Newburyport *Impartial Herald*. He published an equally odd and original book, called *A Pickle for the Knowing Ones; or, Plain Truths in a Homespun Dress,* full of meandering observations on his own life and times. "I—I—me T Dexter of N Port," he wrote to the newspaper, his favorite forum, "Desires Any man or men on the gloube to Exseeds me as to what I have rote in my Littel book . . ."

GLEASON'S PICTORIAL

TWO GENTLEMEN *FROM*

Evenings he was rarely sober, his family life became a shambles, and soon he had attracted a crew of odd-ball companions—including his own poet laureate. Eventually he purchased the Jackson mansion, filled the grounds with statues of historical figures he admired (see next page), and held there—in splendid ceremony—a rehearsal of his own funeral.

Even in his own time, the Dexter legend was larger than life-size. People called him "Lord," and he accepted the title, laughing a little both at himself and those who laughed at him. "Ime the first Lord in the younited States of Amercay," he wrote. "I don't desier the sound but to pleas the peopel at Large—Let it gou to brak the way—it dus for A sortment to help a good Lafe . . ." Sometimes it was difficult to know who was laughing loudest. Dexter kept a lion in his back yard, but he charged ninepence admission. It was said that he had sent shiploads of coal to Newcastle and of warming pans to the West Indies, but the coal arrived during a miners' strike and the warming pans were converted into ladles for sugar-processing while Dexter reaped the profits. For years after his death, the children of Newburyport are supposed to have chanted a little rhyme:

> Dexter is a smart old man;
> Try and catch him if you can.

Dexter, as W. Lloyd Warner might have put it, was "upward mobile." Some inner warp and tension gave him the energy to leap spectacularly above his station, a rise that was one day to become commonplace in the "younited States of Amercay," but was a new thing then. He was not wholly equal to it, and his wits somewhat deserted him. But the more John P. Marquand meditated on the matter, the less certain he was that Dexter's oddness was the sum of the story. Not only was Lord Timothy less of a fool than he let on, he may have seemed more natural in his own time than he does in ours. It was Federal America—that "bizarre but often beautiful historical climate," as Marquand calls it —which made him what he was. Newburyport was a boom town. Few of the *riche* were not *nouveau*, and gentility was everywhere a recent acquisition. Nothing disappears more quickly, and nothing is harder for the historian to reconstruct, than the sense of historical normality, of what was usual and what was exceptional. As Marquand looked back at the Newburyport of his own youth, and put down on paper this matchless portrait of its sights and sounds and smells, he saw it was in many ways closer to Dexter's than either is to the present—a vanished world, indescribable to someone who has not experienced it—and the thought was borne in on him that "the essence is always lost; in the end the dead past will bury its dead."

And so John Marquand wrote, in his last book, what might almost be the graceful bow across the years of one Newburyport gentleman to another, so far apart in birth and breeding, so far apart in time. It was almost as though the novelist of manners had not wanted to depart before saying that in the end rank and class count for less than we imagine, and that even in his own town's most gaudy and disreputable citizen something inner, human, and unique resided.

—*Eric Larrabee*

The eccentric Timothy Dexter finally found a sympathetic biographer in his fellow townsman, novelist John Marquand

NEWBURYPORT

A contemporary lithograph of "Lord" Timothy Dexter's mansion and museum will be found on the next page.

The memory of Lord Dexter and his works would not be so vivid as it is if a publisher had not been so enterprising as to bring out an engraving of Lord Dexter's house and grounds in 1810, four years after the owner's demise. This aquatint has always been a treasured item in Newburyport and among other collectors of Americana. Luckily for the Dexter legend, but also because curiosity regarding the late citizen was already becoming intense, a lithographic copy was published between 1838 and 1850. . . .

The print is a detailed elevation of the house and grounds of the Dexter property as they existed in His Lordship's lifetime. . . . A high arch has been erected before [the] door, on which stand the three figures of the Presidents of the United States: General Washington in the center, flanked by Messrs. Adams and Jefferson. There are other arches to right and left, that support figures of lions and soldiers. Then among these main decorations, rising above small trees and shrubbery, appear a profusion of tall columns, each one a base for some other figure, here an Indian, there a goddess or a famous statesman. . . .

In the year 1801 . . . Mr. Dexter evolved, assuredly with the help of a handful of his better-educated admirers, a plan for constructing for the benefit of the world at large a museum containing the life-sized figures of men and women famous in mythology and history. . . . At first the wooden personages were to

be as follows: "The 3 presidents, Doctor Franklin John hen Cock, and Mr. hamelton and Rouffous king and John Jea—2 grenadars on the top of the hous, 4 Lions below; 1 Eagel *is* on the Coupulow, one Lamb to lay down with one of the Lions—one younecorne, one Dogg, Addam and Eave in the Garden—one horse. The houll is not concluded as yet—Dexter's Mouseum." . . .

Several of Lord Dexter's more thoughtful contemporaries, in reviewing this supreme piece of exhibitionism, have held it as the final proof of a mental disorder. . . . It is difficult not to agree that Mr. Dexter was very confused, but . . . there is unexpected lucidity in his actions. It can be that his plan

was part of a commercial scheme. . . . he was a heavy investor in that modern project, the Essex-Merrimack toll bridge. . . . Dexter, in his anxiety to improve High Street, displayed an intense desire to get more traffic moving along this thoroughfare, which was the way to his Essex-Merrimack Bridge. If he could make his house and grounds a wonder that would attract travelers journeying north, it would increase bridge tolls and defray the expenses of his decorations. He always possessed, in his most depressed moments, the instincts of a showman.

—John P. Marquand, Timothy Dexter Revisited, *Little, Brown and Company.* © *1960 by John P. Marquand*

On a blizzardy April morning in 1892, fifty armed men surrounded a cabin on Powder River in which two accused cattle rustlers had been spending the night. The first rustler was shot as he came down the path for the morning bucket of water; he was dragged over the doorstep by his companion, to die inside. The second man held out until afternoon, when the besiegers fired the house. Driven out by the flames, he went down with twenty-eight bullets in him. He was left on the bloodstained snow with a **card** pinned to his shirt, reading: "Cattle thieves, beware!"

So far the affair follows the standard pattern of frontier heroics, a pattern popularized by Owen Wister and justified to some extent by the facts of history if you don't look too closely: strong men on a far frontier, in the absence of law, make their own law for the protection of society, which generally approves.

Thus runs the cliché, but in Wyoming this time it went awry. In the first place the attackers were not crude frontiersmen taking the law into their own hands. They were men of means and education, predominantly eastern, who really should have known better; civilized men, at home in drawing rooms and familiar with Paris. Two were Harvard classmates of the year '78, the one a Boston blue blood, the other a member of a Wall Street banking family. Hubert E. Teschemacher and Fred DeBillier had come west after graduation to hunt elk, as so many gilded youths from both sides of the Atlantic were doing; had fallen in love with the country; and had remained as partners in a half-million-dollar ranching enterprise.

Our fifty vigilantes were truly a strange company to ride through the land slaughtering people. The instigators dominated the cattle business and the affairs of the former territory, which had recently been elevated to statehood, and more than half of them had served in the legislature. Their leader, Major Frank Wolcott, was a fierce little pouter pigeon of a man, a Kentuckian lately of the Union Army, whose brother was United States senator from Colorado. Accompanying the party as surgeon was a socially prominent Philadelphian, Dr. Charles Bingham Penrose, who had come to Wyoming for his health. It was not improved by his experiences.

These gentlemen had no thought of the danger to themselves as they set out, without benefit of the law, to liquidate their enemies. Convinced of their own righteousness, they expected nine-tenths of the people of Wyoming to be on their side, and they even looked for a popular uprising to assist them. Instead, thirty-six hours after their sanguinary victory on Powder River, they were surrounded in their turn by an enraged horde of citizens, and just missed being lynched

a band of respectable cattle barons

—and barely escaped with their lives

COUNTY WAR

By HELENA HUNTINGTON SMITH

themselves. They were saved only by the intervention of the President of the United States, who ordered federal troops to their aid. But it wasn't quite the usual scene of the cavalry riding to the rescue at the end of the movie, for while the cattlemen were snatched from imminent death, they were also arrested for the murder of the two men and marched off in custody of the troops—the latter, from the commanding officer on down, making clear their personal opinion that they regretted the rescue.

So ended the Johnson County War—tragic, bizarre, unbelievable. It was all a sequel to the great beef bonanza, which began around 1880. The cattle boom combined the most familiar features of the South Sea Bubble and the 1929 bull market—such as forty per cent dividends that would never cease—with some special features of its own—such as a rash of adventuring English Lords and Honorables, free grass, and the blessings of "natural increase" provided by the prolific Texas cow. A man could grow rich without his lifting a finger.

Instead of the old-style cow outfit with its headquarters in a dugout and a boss who ate beef, bacon, and beans, there were cattle companies with offices in Wall Street, London, or Edinburgh; champagne parties; thoroughbred racing on the plains; and younger sons who were shipped out west to mismanage great ranches at fancy salaries. In a raw new city sprawled along the Union Pacific tracks, the Cheyenne Club boasted the best steward of any club in the United States, and its members were drawn from a roster of aristocracy on both sides of the Atlantic. Burke's Peerage and the Social Register mingled, though not intimately, with common cowhands from Texas, but only the latter knew anything about cattle.

To be sure, some of what they knew was a trifle shady: they knew how to handle a long rope and a running iron; how to brand a maverick right out from under the noses of the lords. But the mavericks, unbranded animals of uncertain ownership, were rather casually regarded anyhow; "finders keepers" was the unwritten rule which had governed their disposition in the early days, and they had been a source of controversy and bloodshed throughout the history of the West. While they were now claimed by the big cattle companies, the Texas cowboys were not impressed.

The boom crashed into ruin in the awful winter of 1886-87. Snow fell and drifted and thawed and froze and fell again, clothing the ground with an iron

A Necktie Party *was the title given to this sketch by Charles M. Russell of summary Far Western justice and its somber, deliberate executioners. At least one such lynching was a part of the prologue to the Johnson County War.*

sheath of white on which a stagecoach could travel and through which no bovine hoof could paw for grass; and since the plains were heavily overstocked and the previous summer had been hot and dry, there was no grass anyway. Moaning cattle wandered into the outskirts of towns, trying to eat frozen garbage and the tar paper off the eaves of the shacks; and when the hot sun of early summer uncovered the fetid carcasses piled in the creek bottoms, the bark of trees and brush was gnawed as high as a cow could reach. Herd losses averaged fifty per cent, with ninety per cent for unacclimated southern herds, and some moral revulsion set in, even the Cheyenne *Daily Sun* remarking that a man who turned animals out on a barren plain without food or shelter would suffer loss of respect of the community in which he lived.

Meanwhile there were gloomy faces at the Cheyenne Club. "Cheer up, boys," quipped the bartender across the street, setting out a row of glasses, "the books won't freeze."

In the heyday of the beef bonanza, herds had been bought and sold by "book count," based on a back-of-an-envelope calculation of "natural increase," with no pother about a tally on the range. As the day of reckoning dawned, it turned out that many big companies had fewer than half the number of cattle claimed on their books. Now the terrible winter cut this half down to small fractions; faraway directors, grown glacial as the weather, hinted that blizzards were the fault of their underlings in Cheyenne; while the few surviving cows, instead of giving birth to sextuplets as was their clear duty, produced a correspondingly diminished calf crop to fatten on the gorgeous grass that sprang up after the snows.

In their bitterness, the cattlemen believed that the damned thieves were to blame. Obsessed with this idea, they now proceeded to bring upon themselves an epidemic of stealing without parallel in the West. At least that was what they called it, though to a cool-headed observer from Nebraska it looked more like "the bitter conflict which has raged incessantly between large and small owners."

In fact it was even more. For Wyoming in the nineties shared the outlook of that decade everywhere else; a decade of economic and moral monopoly, when righteousness belonged exclusively to the upper class, along with the means of production; a decade when the best people simply could not be wrong. The best people in this case were the Wyoming Stock Growers Association and their several rich and prominent eastern friends, and the climate of opinion they breathed was startlingly revealed in the hanging of Jim Averill and Cattle Kate. When the cattlemen shed crocodile tears because thieves went unwhipped,

they forgot that thieves were not the worst to go free. At least six persons were shot or hanged in the years before the final flare-up, but not one person was ever brought to trial for the crimes—not even in the case of Jim Averill and the woman whose real name was Ella, who were hanged on the Sweetwater in 1889.

Averill and Ella ran a log-cabin saloon and road ranch up a desolate little valley off the Sweetwater, and they were nuisances. The man was articulate and a Populist of sorts, and had attacked the big cattlemen in a letter to the local press; the woman was a cowboys' prostitute who took her pay in stolen cattle. From this, aristocratic Dr. Penrose could argue later that "she had to die for the good of the country."

Die she did, with her paramour, at the end of a rope thrown over a tree limb and swung out over a gulch. There were three eyewitnesses to the abduction and one to the actual hanging, and a coroner's jury named four prominent cattlemen among the perpetrators. But before the case reached the grand jury three of the witnesses had vanished and the fourth had conveniently died. Afterward two of the men whose hands were filthy from this affair continued to rub elbows with the fastidious Teschemaker on the executive committee of the Stock Growers Association, and nauseating jokes about the last moments of Kate were applauded at the Cheyenne Club. Even Owen Wister joined in the applause, noting in his diary for October 12, 1889: "Sat yesterday in smoking car with one of the gentlemen indicted [*sic*] for lynching the man and the woman. He seemed a good solid citizen and I hope he'll get off."

The association tightened its blacklist. In a cattle

economy where cows were the only means of getting ahead, the cowboys had long been forbidden to own a brand or a head of stock on their own, lest they be tempted to brand a maverick. Now more and more of them were "blackballed" on suspicion from all lawful employment within the territory. Likewise the association made the rules of the range, ran the roundups to suit itself, and kept out the increasing number of people it didn't like; hence many small stockmen, suspect of misbehavior by their very smallness, were also relegated to a shady no man's land outside the law.

If you call a man a thief, treat him like a thief, and deprive him of all chance to earn a living honestly, he will soon oblige you by becoming a thief.

By 1890 a thin colony of blackballed cowboys had settled on the rivers and creeks of Johnson County and were waging war with rope and running iron on the big outfits. Then early in 1892 a group calling themselves the Northern Wyoming Farmers' and Stockgrowers' Association announced in the press their intention of holding an independent roundup, in defiance of the state law and the Wyoming Stock Growers Association. This was provocative, insolent, outrageous if you like; it was hardly the furtive behavior of ordinary thieves.

Also announced in the press were the names of two foremen for what was now being called the "shotgun roundup." One was a Texan, known as a skilled cowhand, who was lightning with a gun. His name was Nathan D. Champion.

Meanwhile the storied walls of the Cheyenne Club beheld the amazing spectacle of nineteenth century gentlemen plotting wholesale murder. The declared object of their expedition was the "extermination"— not "arrest," but "extermination"—of various undesirable persons in the northern part of the state. The death list stood at seventy. In addition to a hard core of nineteen most-wanted rustlers, it almost certainly included a large number who were merely thought to be too close to the rustler faction, among them the sheriff of Johnson County and the three county commissioners.

This incredible project was fully known in advance to Acting Governor Amos W. Barber, to United States Senators Joseph M. Carey and Francis E. Warren, and to officials of the Union Pacific Railroad, whose consent to run a special train was obtained; and none of whom found anything questionable in the undertaking. Twenty-five hired gunfighters from Texas raised the manpower complement to fifty, since the local cowboys were thoroughly disaffected and would not have pulled a trigger for their employers. A smart Chicago newsman, Sam T. Clover, had heard about the impending necktie party and was in Cheyenne determined to get the story for the *Herald*. He and a local reporter were taken along just as though the expedition were legal; it apparently had not occurred to the planners that they were inviting witnesses to murder.

They got started the afternoon of April 5, on board a train loaded with men, arms, equipment, horses, and three supply wagons. An overnight run landed them in Casper, two hundred miles to the northwest, where they descended, saddled their horses, and were off before the townspeople were up—except for enough of the latter to start talk. Their objective was Buffalo, the county seat of Johnson County, but when they arrived at a friendly ranch on the second night, they received new intelligence which determined them to change their course: Nate Champion and possibly a good catch of other rustlers were at a cabin on the Middle Fork of Powder River, only twelve miles away. They decided to detour and finish this group off before proceeding to Buffalo.

Rumors have come down to us of the drinking and dissension that accompanied this decision: faced with the actuality of shooting trapped men in a cabin the next morning, stomachs began to turn over, and three members of the party pulled out, including the doctor and the local newsman. But that night the main body rode on to the attack, through one of the worst April

CONTINUED ON PAGE 74

REVEILLE *on*
EAST 75*th* STREET
or
Roughing It with the Girl Scouts of 1918
in a Manhattan Mansion

Cooking took place in Mrs. Macy's ample fireplace, leaving the kitchen untouched. Leafy boughs and the Girl Scout flag adorn what was evidently the command post, where two leaders, Mrs. James J. Storrow of Boston (left) and Mrs. Josephine Bacon, editor of the Girl Scout magazine, are studying photographs. Reconnaissance for tomorrow's operations? No one remembers.

If there is any axiom about pioneering, it is this: the further back one goes in history, the tougher it was. Where Grandpa hacked his way through the wilderness, we ride the throughway. Father, he is happy to tell the world, worked harder than you. Before you new recruits joined up, one learns in any organization, life in this outfit was infinitely more rugged. We trust that this point is abundantly clear because, in honor of its forthcoming fiftieth anniversary, we publish herewith a possibly confusing glimpse of Girl Scouting back in the pioneer days.

The time was October, 1918, when America faced not only imperial Germany but a style in women's dress which, had it continued, might have depopulated the land in a generation. The place was not a comfortable modern forest but a huge city mansion at 4 East 75th Street, New York. It was empty of furniture and its owner, Mrs. V. Everit Macy, had loaned it to the Scouts as a campsite. The girls in the pictures, which were made on glass plates, were among twenty-seven student leaders taking part in one of the organization's first national training courses in Scouting and youthful war work.

According to an official journal kept by one "Marion C. Moreland, Scribe," the girls had a lovely time, struggling from reveille at 5:30 to taps at 9:30 to overcome their embarrassingly urban environment. They slept on army cots and drilled in the empty ballroom, and their cooking—which ran heavily to beans, bacon, and flapjacks—took place over the open fire, leaving Mrs. Macy's elaborate ovens cold and untouched. There were drills, calisthenics, trips to the Natural History Museum and a deer park in White Plains, marching in Central Park, and lectures and singing at night.

Girl Scouting has grown tremendously—there is one potential cookie merchant among every seven American girls today—since its founding in 1912. The entrepreneur was the remarkable Juliette Gordon Low, a friend and admirer of Sir Robert Baden-Powell, founder of Boy Scouting and, with his sister, of England's Girl Guides. As they celebrate Mrs. Low's recent centenary, and her achievements in turning girls into healthy young women, modern Scouts can find, perhaps, one extra satisfaction in these pictures: Grandma had better not say too much about the hardships of being a Girl Scout in her day.

Scout leader trainees stand at attention as smartly as possible, considering the uniform, while inspection takes place. The troops slept on army cots and, to simulate frontier conditions, eschewed the use of Mrs. Macy's electricity. The problem of the electric front-door buzzer was solved by substituting a cowbell.

Tea and singing came at four in the afternoon, followed by drill. "In the evening," according to the scribe's official notes, "Miss Kingsbury taught games, Tag, Japanese Tag, Whip Tag, Three Deep, Four Deep, and Snatch." Then, after singing a round of folk songs, the girls retired at taps to the murmuring pine-paneled rooms upstairs.

55

Sam
The Mayor
Jones

When Samuel Milton Jones, right, the sucker-rod magnate who became mayor of Toledo, attempted to apply the social gospel of Jesus to city government as well as to the management of his own plant, he was branded a dangerous radical. His philosophy of reform was epitomized in the question: "Shall we have the Golden Rule of all the people or the rule of cash by a few people?"

Jones *v*

In Toledo a civic crusade

against a famed evangelis

By WILLIAM G

When the Protestant ministers of Toledo, Ohio, voted almost unanimously to invite the fiery and widely renowned southern evangelist, Samuel Porter Jones, to lead a month-long crusade in the spring of 1899, it was apparent to everyone that the salvation of souls was not their only aim. However loudly they might proclaim a great campaign to regenerate the city's flagging spiritual life, they seemed somehow more concerned with the outcome of the mayoralty election that was to be held while Sam Jones was in town. Inspired by his loud, folksy humor and fundamentalist faith, they hoped to drive out of office a mayor who frankly and stubbornly refused to enforce the existing laws against gambling, slot machines, drinking, prostitution, and —perhaps worst of all—Sabbathbreaking. By a strange coincidence, the offending mayor's name also happened to be Sam Jones.

Mayor Samuel Milton Jones, nicknamed "Golden Rule" Jones, had not earned his sobriquet in jest, for in his own way he had sincerely tried to put the social gospel of Jesus into practice. Unfortunately, his views on Christianity were a little novel for his time. That the Mayor professed to believe in and run the city government on the basis of the Golden Rule—"Do unto others as you would have them do unto you"— struck the ministers as sacrilegious hypocrisy, if not Red revolution. "Ministers almost to a man feel betrayed and outraged," said one of their principal

spokesmen. "They feel that the one great thing to be settled first is: Shall Toledo obey the law?"

The contest that resulted was one of the most ironic and yet significant episodes in the long and colorful history of revivalism and social reform in America. For while the two Sam Joneses were outspoken advocates of Christianity as a philosophy of life, they were absolutely at odds in their solutions to the burning social issues of the day. But more important, their struggle dramatized the irreconcilable conflict within the incipient Progressive movement between the evangelicals, who felt that reform must begin with the individual, and the social gospelers, who believed that it must begin with society. In a sense, the choice which faced the citizens of Toledo epitomized the one which faced the whole nation at the turn of the century.

Mayor Sam M. Jones was born in Ty Mawr, Wales, in 1846; he was a year older than the evangelist Sam P. Jones, who was born in Alabama and raised in the hill country of northern Georgia. Both men came from devout Methodist homes; the evangelist remembered how his grandmother had "read the Bible through thirty-seven times, on her knees." Migrating to America in 1849, the Mayor's family had settled on a tenant farm in upper New York State; at fourteen, he left home to seek his fortune in the newly opened oil fields of Pennsylvania and Ohio. The evangelist, however, was brought up in somewhat better circumstances. His father was a successful lawyer

Sam
The Preacher
Jones

Samuel Porter Jones, left, the free-swinging Georgia evangelist, was one of rugged individualism's most vocal advocates. "God projected this world on the root-hog-or-die-poor principle," said he. "If the hog, or man either, don't root, let him die." One of the most sought-after speakers of his day, Jones transformed his supercharged revival meetings into live political crusades.

COLLECTION OF THE REV. WALT HOLCOMB

s. *Jones*

natched the popular mayor

—both with the same name

IcLOUGHLIN

and businessman, who served as a captain in Robert E. Lee's Army of Northern Virginia. Like him, the preacher-to-be set out to become a lawyer. But his promising career was soon blighted by an unquenchable addiction to the bottle.

Thanks to his mother's prayers and a rigorously Calvinistic upbringing, Mayor Jones was a lifelong teetotaler. He worked hard in the oil fields, and gradually saved enough money to invest in a successful oil company in Lima, Ohio. Eventually, this concern was bought out by John D. Rockefeller's burgeoning Standard Oil Company; with his proceeds Jones opened a small factory in Toledo. Here he manufactured a mechanical contrivance called a sucker rod, used in drilling for oil, which he had invented and patented himself. It was a good invention, and as the demand for it grew, so did Jones's financial status: the familiar American saga of rags to riches had been repeated once more.

Meanwhile Sam P. Jones was saved from alcoholism by a promise he made to his dying father in the year 1872. Once delivered from sin and drink, the reformed lawyer decided to enter the ministry. Starting his new career with "a wife and one child, a bobtail pony and eight dollars in cash," he traveled as a Methodist circuit rider in some of the poorest counties of northern Georgia for the next eight years. While the future mayor of Toledo converted sucker rods into cash, the future revivalist converted rednecks into God-fearing

churchgoers. Both men were too able, forceful, and energetic to remain long in obscurity, though it was hardly inevitable that their paths should have crossed in such dramatic fashion when they were at the height of their respective careers. Or was it?

In 1885, the Georgia preacher was asked to conduct a revival meeting for the Methodist churches of Nashville, Tennessee. Jones made such a sensational success of it that he abandoned pastoral work for evangelism. His handsome face, fiery rhetoric, and missionary zeal soon made him the most popular revivalist in the South. A slim, dark, forthright man, his deep-set eyes flashed indignation at one moment and twinkled with amusement the next. Unlike his plump, benign, walrus-mustached counterpart in Toledo, however, the evangelist did not enjoy good health and suffered often from stomach trouble and spells of exhaustion. Yet his passion for preaching drove him to constant activity. If Sam M. Jones could claim that his oil-pumping invention was advancing America's material progress, Sam P. Jones could fairly have claimed two innovations in urban revival techniques that were, in their own way, equally as important. Not only was Jones the first evangelist in America to make revival meet-

William G. McLoughlin is associate professor of history at Brown University. This article is based on his Modern Revivalism: Charles Grandison Finney to Billy Graham, *published and copyright, 1959, by the Ronald Press Company.*

57

An enlightened industrialist, Mayor Jones established the "Golden Rule Park" next to his factory for his employees.

ings as entertaining and applause-conscious as the theater, but he was also the first one to turn revival campaigns into civic-reform crusades.

Early in his career Jones began to tell his revival audiences, "Fun is the next best thing to religion." "When I get up to preach," he said, "I just knock out the bung and let nature cut her capers." Newspaper reporters noted with surprise that Jones had his audience howling in fits of irrepressible laughter more often than he had them in tears or terror. "We have been clamoring for forty years for a learned ministry," he would say, "and we have got it today and the church is deader than it ever has been in history. Half of the literary preachers in this town are A.B.'s, Ph.D.'s, D.D.'s, LL.D.'s, and A.S.S.'s." He often parodied the old hymn "Shall Jesus Bear the Cross Alone" to scold the hypocrites who came to church twice a year at Christmas and Easter, and then only to show off their new clothes. "The way you sing it," he told these lip-service Christians, "is

> *Shall Jesus bear the cross alone,*
> *And all the world go free?*
> *No, there's a cross for everyone,*
> *And an Easter bonnet for me."*

It is not surprising that during the summer months, Evangelist Jones made a handsome income lecturing on the lyceum and Chautauqua circuits where he competed successfully with such platform artists as Mark Twain, Josh Billings, and Artemus Ward. By 1899 he had become as striking a testimonial to the American myth of success as his entrepreneurial namesake in Toledo; his earnings from lecturing and revivals averaged thirty thousand dollars a year, a large sum in those income-tax-free years.

Strangely enough, businessman Sam M. Jones himself underwent a religious conversion in these same years, but of a very different nature. Shortly after he moved to Toledo in 1892, he came under the influence of the Reverend George D. Herron, a Congregational minister from Grinnell, Iowa, whose flaming oratory and burning interest in social problems made him one of the most controversial and influential religious leaders in the Midwest. Herron, one of the first of America's social gospelers, disagreed vigorously with the accepted Protestant ethic of the Gilded Age which taught that poverty, crime, and most other social problems were due to lack of character, will power, or integrity among the lower classes. Before he heard Herron, the self-made sucker-rod magnate would have heartily endorsed this viewpoint. He would have agreed, before 1892, with the new social Darwinian philosophy preached by men like Herbert Spencer. The evolutionary principle of survival of the fittest, they said, gave scientific endorsement to the ethic of rugged individualism that Evangelist Jones espoused in these words: "God projected this world on the root-hog-or-die-poor principle. If the hog, or man either, don't root, let him die."

But after he had heard the social gospel of George Herron, the whole outlook of the rich young manufacturer was permanently altered. Herron preached that the heart of the gospel Jesus taught was the ideal of social justice—it was nothing less than the coming of the Kingdom of God on earth:

Except the state be born again, except it be delivered from pagan doctrines of law and government, from commercial and polite conceptions of its functions . . . it cannot see the divine social kingdom. . . . The supremacy of the law of self-interest is the conclusion of Herbert Spencer's materialistic philosophy. It is the principle upon which Cain slew his brother. . . . the law of self-interest is the eternal falsehood which mothers all social and private woes; for sin is pure individualism—the assertion of self against God and humanity. . . .

Herron's views were re-enforced in Jones's mind by his experience with the great depression of 1893 when he saw able-bodied men in Toledo literally begging for work to keep their families from starving. Forsaking his belief in rugged individualism and the laissez faire system based upon it, he became, like Herron, a Christian socialist.

While his business friends shook their heads and the community clucked its tongue, Jones announced in 1895 that from that time forward he would run his sucker-rod factory strictly "upon the basis of the Golden Rule." He had arrived at this decision after reading Herron's book, *The New Redemption*, in which he found this striking maxim: "He who builds a mercantile establishment upon the basis of the Golden Rule is a greater and wiser philanthropist than he who founds hospitals for the poor out of the gains of selfishness."

To implement this principle in his own "mercantile establishment," Jones began by cutting the regular work day from ten hours to eight, at the same time raising his minimum wage from $1.25 a day (the prevailing rate in all factories) to $2.00. He then announced that every worker in his factory would receive a Christmas bonus of five per cent of his yearly salary on the grounds that they all had a right to share in the annual profits of the company. He instituted an employee sickness and unemployment insurance plan to which the company and the workers donated equal amounts. He purchased a plot of ground next to the factory to make a park where the workers could spend their lunch hours. It was called "Golden Rule Park." At one end of it he built a children's playground and at the other, a bandstand where weekly band concerts were held. He helped his employees to form their own brass band. He brought popular speakers on political and economic subjects from all over the country to address his workers, either in the park or in an auditorium which he added to the factory. He established an employee restaurant and had hot meals served there at a flat rate of fifteen cents each although they cost him twenty-one cents each. An annual company picnic was organized in an attempt to break down the barrier between the white-collar clerks, the shopworkers, and the management. In addition, Jones was one of the first employers in the country to give his factory workers a regular summer vacation with pay. He also gave his employees shares of stock in the company to make them part-owners. Though all of these reforms seem commonplace now, in 1895 they were considered the height of folly and radicalism.

But the reform which heaped upon him the ultimate in ridicule was his decision to abolish the use of supervisory bosses and timekeepers in the factory and to leave every worker free to keep his own time sheet and work at his own pace. Although he was called a muddle-headed visionary, Jones knew what he was doing. "Most manufacturers," he said, "keep about eight out of every ten dollars which their employees earn for them. I keep only about seven, and so they call me 'Golden Rule' Jones."

Of course, a few workers cheated him; some grum-

TOLEDO *Blade*, MARCH 22, 1899

This cartoon from a Republican paper played up the Independent mayor's "links" with gamblers and saloonkeepers.

bled at the burden of responsibility thrust upon them; the company picnics failed to break down the social barriers between the white-collar and blue-collar workers. But on the whole the experiment was a success. The Acme Sucker Rod Company continued to thrive, and in 1899 Jones could state publicly, "After nearly four years, I am pleased to say that the Golden Rule works. It is perfectly practical and worthy of a trial. But my experience has shown me that it is a *social*, not an industrial rule, and no *one* can truly live the Golden Rule until all live it."

While Revivalist Jones had probably never heard of George Herron nor "Golden Rule" Jones until he received the invitation to preach in Toledo in 1899, he was not unaware of the glaring social problems of American industrial and urban life. Like most Americans, the evangelist was shocked at the record of crime and corruption which the muckraking journalists were beginning to set before the public eye. He was appalled at the effrontery of political bosses who robbed the public treasury of millions, who corrupted the democratic process by buying votes or stuffing ballot boxes, who invaded even the legislatures and the courts with bribery, boodle, and blackmail. And too, he shared the public's growing concern with the problems of anarchism, socialism, and communism, which were associated in most people's minds with the growth of labor unions and the increase in foreign immigration.

In his revival sermons Jones often emphasized the

CONTINUED ON PAGE 84

59

sant miguel capoltepan

sanfrancisco tlotopan

s. mia

Camino Real Copan

Iztela

Haltemaquia

sanctiago tonalapan

plaza zpzom

Sancta maria acumo

Sant pedro vertenilan

en San Jua tututla

Sant estevan quauhteno

The King's Census: 1577

Philip II's *cédula real* evoked from his overseas domains
vivid picture-maps of life in Spanish America

By IRMA REED WHITE
U. S. Bureau of the Census

Throughout recorded history the marks of the empire builder have been a passion for order and a determination to allow not even the farthest corners of his realm to go unsupervised; the story of Christianity itself begins in the midst of a census decreed for tax purposes by a Roman emperor. To this rule Philip II of Spain was no exception. The 400-year-old maps reproduced here and on the next two pages were drawn in compliance with Philip's *cédula real,* or royal decree, of 1577 ordering an enumeration of his subjects in New Spain, which then included modern Mexico and parts of Louisiana, Florida, New Mexico, and Arizona.

Philip had drawn up a list of fifty very detailed questions to be answered by his local officials. In addition to population figures, he requested from each pueblo information on housing; an appraisal of the comparative health of the natives before and after the coming of the Spaniards (it seems to have declined); facts on how conquered and conquerors earned their living in trading, farming, or business; information on whether grapes or olives could be grown; and a progress report on the conversion of the Indians. In these respects the questionnaire of 1577 resembled earlier ones sent to New Spain, but in one important regard it was different. Question 10 requested: "Show by a map the situation of the pueblo whether it be of high or low elevation, or level. Sketch in the streets and plazas and important places such as monasteries. Show *north* on the map." The resulting documents—now in the Archives of the Indies in Seville—give us a glimpse of America as it looked just when things were getting started. They are reproduced here in color for the first time.

Of the 135 pueblos that responded to the royal order, relatively few appear to have submitted maps, and those that were received varied a good deal. Some, like the one opposite, were elaborate and painstaking; others were crude and devoid even of place names. They were drawn on coarse agave paper made from the maguey plant. For ink the artists used cochineal, a dye made from the dried bodies of wood lice that infest cactus plants; the colors—crimson, orange, scarlet—were determined by the species of cactus on which the insects fed.

Some of the maps portray graphically one of imperial Spain's major aims: the attempt to wed native and Spanish cultures. For example, each pueblo shown on the Cuzcatlan map (page 63) combines the name of a Christian saint with that of an Aztec hero, and at the bottom, the *picota* of San Geronimo faces the pueblo church. Further, the sworn census witnesses often include both Spanish recorders and Aztec interpreters. In such ways these maps are vivid pictures of life in sixteenth-century Spanish America.

In the map of Tetela in the Bishopric of Tlaxcala, the large buildings are churches, surrounded by small adobe Indian huts. In the plaza to the left of the largest church appears a picota, *a place of pagan ceremonies. The population—450 tax-paying males—is written in at bottom. West is designated by a setting sun at the right-hand edge.*

61

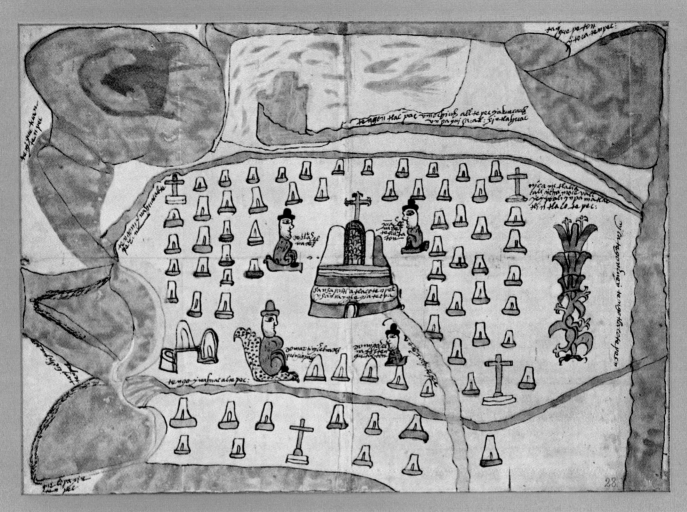

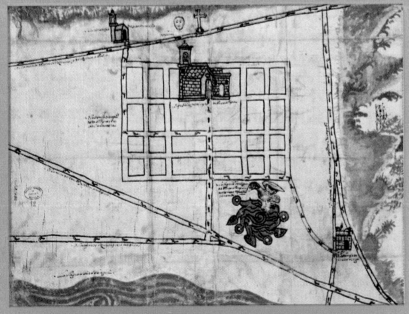

The map of San Sebastian Tlacotepec (above) shows the four governing officials of the Aztec settlement grouped around the church. The small structures are the houses of the 74 inhabitants, ringed about completely by a canal. The church dominates the map of Chicualoapa (left); on which the scrivener indicated the houses only by their plots. The crest is an Aztec symbol surmounted by a chicuatotl, a local bird that gave the town its name. The district of Cuzcatlan, at right, is crossed with streams, the confluences of which are shown as swirls. Hoofprints mark the highways. In the central settlement, the church of San Juan Evangelista Cuzcatlan stands in a plaza with its fountain (fuente) and gallows (orca). The squares at bottom are piles of salt from the marshes around one of the pueblos. Four suns indicate the principal points of the compass, east being the full-face sun at the top. The remaining symbols bordering the map are Aztec designations of pueblos subject to Cuzcatlan.

San martin maxaltepa
San pedro tetlapa
San fran.con ramari oriente
Sanlago tlilapan
aquipa de lambach
banda del sur es jun
dicion de teutitlan

Santa maria xiultula chimalguacan

camino

San Jhoan Evangelista cuxcatlan
plaça fuentes
plaça
orca
camino

Santa maria costilpan

camino

San Jhoan Julco

San pedro xoxtepec

San geronimo alindando de tuas

plaça
poniente

camino real

19

MAD OLD MAN *from* MASSACHUSETTS

How gnarled, upright ex-President John Quincy Adams broke

the South's gag rule in Congress and at last won popular applause

By LAWRENCE LADER

After his defeat for re-election to the Presidency in 1828, John Quincy Adams cloistered himself in his Quincy, Massachusetts, home and wrote in anguish, "I have no plausible motive for wishing to live when everything that I foresee and believe of futurity makes death desirable, and when I have the clearest indications that it is near at hand." Bitterly, Adams resigned himself to the political graveyard, complaining, "My whole life has been a succession of disappointments. I can scarcely recollect a single instance of success to anything that I ever undertook."

Short, paunchy, and almost completely bald, Adams was old before his time. Infirmities overwhelmed him. His hand shook almost uncontrollably when he wrote. He complained about his "smarting, bloodshot eyes," so weak and inflamed that rheumy tears often trickled from the corners. His voice, always shrill, tended to crack. He slept little and badly, and his diary was filled with continual laments of "disturbed, unquiet sleep—full of tossings." His temper was increasingly short: "Fierce as ten furies, terrible as hell," Andrew Johnson described it. And Adams admitted in his diary, "I have need of a perpetual control over passion."

When a group of devoted friends, National Republicans, convinced him to run for Congress in 1830, Adams felt as if he had been born anew. He was sixty-three, a retired President, son of the second President, and one of the nation's last firm links with the Revolution, for Adams as a boy had watched the cannon-smoke roll over Bunker Hill. But it was unprecedented, and remains so today, for a former President to return to the brawling forum of the House. Adams won his election and entered Congress; there he would serve for the next eighteen years, until the end of his life. Instead of the bucolic solitude sought by Washington and other ex-Presidents, Adams would carve out a radical new career. Though he had carefully dodged the slavery issue in the White House, he would now plunge into it almost recklessly, drawing a whirlwind of controversy around his head. No other former President would suffer such abuse, newspapers even branding him the "Mad Man from Massachusetts." And yet, the old Puritan war horse, so aloof as a President, would become the foremost champion of popular liberties, surrounded by a warmth and devotion that had never come to him in the White House.

From birth, John Quincy Adams was steeped in the Puri-

In 1847, shortly before his death, John Quincy Adams (left) sat for this daguerreotype. This account of his tempestuous last years is taken from Lawrence Lader's The Bold Brahmins, *published this month by Dutton.*

tan's tortuous devotion to principle, devoured by the preoccupation with good and evil, molded by his father for public service whose ultimate target was the Presidency. At twenty-six he was appointed Minister to the Netherlands, and nine years later elected to the United States Senate. Madison made him Minister to Russia. Monroe made him his Secretary of State, a position he filled brilliantly from 1817 to 1824, when he won the Presidency from Andrew Jackson in a bitterly fought contest that had to be decided in the House of Representatives. Old John Adams lived to see the family destiny completed, his son in the White House. He died on July 4, 1826, the same day as Jefferson, and the fiftieth anniversary of the Declaration of Independence.

It was the end of an epoch. Only one congressional elector had voted against Monroe in 1820, but John Quincy Adams was a minority President, struggling to hold the National Republicans together. Finally, in 1828, a combination of southern planters and northern Republicans behind Jackson and Calhoun crushed the two northern candidates, Adams and Richard Rush. Slavery was already the hidden issue.

No man had condemned slavery in more blistering words than Adams—"the great and foul stain upon the North American Union!" No man had better gauged the tragic consequences of the Missouri Compromise of 1820. "Oh, if but one man could arise . . . to lay bare in all its nakedness that outrage upon the goodness of God, human slavery," he wrote that year, "now is the time, and this is the occasion, upon which such a man would perform the duties of an angel upon earth!"

It would be sixteen years before Adams would attempt these duties—and even then, inadvertently. In his maiden speech to Congress in 1831, he presented fifteen petitions from citizens of Pennsylvania, praying for abolition of slavery and the slave trade in the nation's capital. Although the petitions caused a bedlam of southern protests, few congressmen, and not even Adams, foresaw the consequences.

By 1834, the petition to Congress, a right guaranteed by the Constitution, had become the major weapon in a well-organized campaign by the American Antislavery Society. As petitions poured upon his desk, Adams presented them in increasing numbers to the House. For all his hatred of slavery, he was still far from an abolitionist. But he doggedly defended the right of petition, and each petition from towns and villages all over New England stirred new debate. Adams and his petitions would soon turn the House into an inferno.

Ironically enough, the petition campaign was de-

veloped by peace-loving Quakers and launched in Essex County, Massachusetts, by the Quaker poet John Greenleaf Whittier. The abolitionists were tireless collectors. One petition, demanding the abolition of slavery in the District of Columbia, carried 130,200 names; another to prohibit slave trade between the states, 23,160; a third to prohibit slavery in United States territories, 21,200; and so on down the line. In Massachusetts, petitions circulated in 1843 to free the slave Latimer drew 51,862 signatures. Dr. Henry Ingersoll Bowditch described "the immense roll of paper" as "about the size of an ordinary barrel." The abolitionist leader Henry B. Stanton estimated that in 1838–39 the American Antislavery Society gathered two million signatures, an impressive percentage of the total population of the United States, even allowing for some inflation of the figures.

In fact, the stacks of petitions were piled so high in the basement of the Capitol that when Albert Bushnell Hart, the Harvard historian, visited there seventy years later he found the janitor still using them to light the fire in his stove.

Adams calmly presented each petition to a fuming House. On one particular day, he introduced fifty separate petitions; not long after, three hundred and fifty. Each interrupted the business of the House, and roused southern representatives to an ever-increasing fury. They had hoped to bury slavery as an issue of debate with the Missouri Compromise. They had even tried to ban abolition literature from the U.S. mails— the bill had passed the House with Jackson's backing, only to fail in the Senate. But here were the abolitionists, exploiting the petition device, forcing the slavery issue into national debate, turning the House into a constant bedlam. As the *Antislavery Bugle* of Salem, Ohio, admitted later, they were determined "to take possession of Congress and turn it into a vast Antislavery Debating Society with the whole country as the audience."

The dominant slavery bloc, which included not only southern representatives but their northern allies, decided to crush these agitators. On May 18, 1836, a committee headed by Henry Laurens Pinckney of South Carolina presented three resolutions, all quickly passed. The key resolution stated that any petition or memorial to Congress relating to slavery should be automatically laid on the table without discussion. It was a sweeping "gag rule" that would be renewed at every session for the next eight years.

Unwittingly, the southern congressmen had caught themselves in a trap of their own making. For by tying the petition gag to the larger issue of constitutional rights, the abolitionists had not only found a common ground on which moderate antislavery men and the extremists could unite against the South, but a way to involve the House in an almost endless and bitter wrangling from which the South had nothing to gain and almost everything to lose. The weakness of the southern position was not only that it abridged the right of petition, but that the gag rule was obviously aimed solely at antislavery spokesmen. Not once did the House use the gag to stop petitions on any other issue.

Adams immediately protested the gag, crying, "I hold the resolution to be a direct violation of the Constitution of the United States, of the rules of this House, and of the rights of my constituents." But he was howled down. The slave bloc had clamped its gag on the nation. Not one petition, not one word of debate on slavery would henceforth be tolerated by the people's representatives!

Adams now took on virtually the entire House in one of the wildest struggles in congressional history. Refusing to be gagged, he resorted to every trick and parliamentary device to bring the slavery issue to the floor. One Washington correspondent described him "creeping through this rule and skipping over that" while the Speaker angrily gaveled him down. Week after week, he infuriated his colleagues with "tit-bit speeches, which were so short and so quickly said that, though they were out of order, nobody could call him to order; and when they did, he would say, 'My speech is done.'"

He would leap to his feet, his face flushed, "throwing himself into the attitude of the veteran gladiator . . .

immovable as a pillar until he has completed his task," another correspondent wrote. He had never been an accomplished speaker, admitting in his diary, "I am so little qualified by nature for an extemporaneous orator that I was at this time not a little agitated by the sound of my own voice." Now his shrill words seemed to explode with new power. His epithets lashed the House unmercifully. One representative, a leading proponent of the gag, was attacked for "emitting a half hour of his rotten breath." Another was branded "the very thickest skull of all New Hampshire." A third, cried Adams, kept "butting his head against the air like a he-goat."

One day Adams presented a petition from 228 women, praying for the abolition of the slave trade in the District of Columbia. When Speaker James K. Polk demanded that its contents be stated, Adams provoked the usual pandemonium, described by the *National Intelligencer*:

ADAMS: I am doing so, Sir.
POLK: Not in the opinion of the Chair.
ADAMS: I was at this point of the petition, "keenly aggrieved by its (slavery's) existence in a part of our country over which Congress possesses exclusive jurisdiction in all cases whatever"—
Cries of "Order! Order!" shook the House.
ADAMS: "Do most earnestly petition your honorable body"—
John Chambers of Kentucky rose to a point of order.
ADAMS: (rushing to complete his sentence before the House drowned him out) "Immediately to abolish slavery in the District of Columbia."

When the Speaker's gavel or the furious chorus of "Order! Order!" stopped him, Adams employed other devices—amending the House journal, or presenting a petition that ingeniously skirted the slavery provisions of the gag rule.

Frequently he even refused to tell the Speaker the contents of a petition, crying, "I refuse to answer because I consider all the proceedings of the House as unconstitutional." Adams in his diary reported that "While speaking these words with loud, distinct and slow articulation, the bawl of 'Order! Order!' resounded again from two thirds of the House. The Speaker, with agonizing lungs, screamed, 'I call upon the House to support me in the execution of my duty.' I then coolly resumed my seat."

In February, 1837, Adams presented a petition from nine Negro women of Fredericksburg, Virginia, not knowing himself whether they were slaves or free. The Speaker immediately tabled it. Adams then announced he was presenting another petition, signed with scrawls and marks. An uproar rose through the House, for no petition from slaves had ever before been presented.

Southern representatives screamed that Adams was destroying the Union; one demanded that he be indicted by the District grand jury for inciting rebellion. The storm continued for three days, Adams cagily helping to whip it up.

Biding his time until the House let him speak, he blandly announced that the petition had nothing to do with freedom. Just the opposite! The slaves had petitioned the House to protect them from the abolitionists lest their welfare be harmed. "It remains," wrote one historian a half century later, "the best and most effective practical joke in the history of Congress."

Since Adams sturdily insisted that his petition battle was based on the freedom of petition, his enemies put him to the test. They sent him a petition, praying Congress that all free Negroes be deported or sold as slaves. Adams methodically presented it. When the citizens of Rocky Mount, Virginia, sent him a petition praying Congress to expel the Honorable John Quincy Adams, he never hesitated to present it.

Such puritanical devotion to principle brought an increasing flood of ferocious letters to his desk. ". . . Your damned guts will be cut out in the dark," warned a Georgia correspondent. "On the first day of May next I promise to cut your throat from ear to ear," threatened an Alabama writer. Nearing his seventy-fourth birthday, still unflinching in his lonely struggle although he complained privately of his "drowsy brain" and "my faculties dropping from me one by one, as the teeth are dropping from my head," Adams already ranked as the nation's most vilified ex-President.

When General Sam Houston's victory over Mexico's Santa Anna on April 21, 1836, stirred to the point of mania the nation's dream of annexing Texas, southern leaders grasped hungrily at this vast, new territory from which they hoped to carve an array of slave states.

The Texas mania, however, seriously alarmed the North, including large segments of the population which had no connection with the abolitionist groups. Dr. William Ellery Channing, the dominant voice of the Unitarian sect, published a scathing tract against annexation which reached an immense audience. Anti-Texas petitions began to flood the House conjointly with abolition ones. Anti-Texas resolutions by the state legislatures came from Massachusetts, Michigan, Ohio, and Vermont.

Although Adams, as President, had twice tried but failed to purchase Texas from Mexico, he was now convinced that the Texas revolution was a plot by Jackson, the plantation owners, and their northern allies. "The Texas land and liberty jobbers," he would soon charge, "had spread the contagion of their land-jobbing traffic all over the free states throughout the Union. Land-jobbing, stock-jobbing, slave-jobbing, rights-of-man-jobbing were all hand in hand, sweeping over the land like a hurricane."

In the closing months of 1837, Adams forced these anti-Texas petitions to the floor, deftly slipping in a number of abolition ones at the same time. Although Speaker Polk struggled to shut him off, Adams got the House floor during the morning hours which were usually consumed in routine business and held it tenaciously each day for three weeks. His one-man campaign and the flood of petitions stalled the Administration; annexation had to be postponed.

Still, the southern bloc kept its gag clamped on the House, although it was slowly losing ground. In 1836, 82 of 117 votes approving the gag rule came from the free states. In 1840, when the gag passed by only 114 to 108, just 28 of the Yeas were from the North.

Even a few southern papers gradually turned against the gag. "It would be establishing a precedent dangerous alike to the liberties of the South or the North," warned the Natchitoches, Louisiana, *Herald* on January 12, 1838.

The lack of unified support even from slavery's opponents intensified Adams' solitary struggle. "He [Benjamin Lundy, a Quaker abolitionist] and the abolitionists generally are constantly urging me to indiscreet movements, which would ruin me and weaken and not strengthen their cause," he wrote on September 2, 1837. ". . . I walk on the edge of a precipice in every step that I take." Two years later he was still complaining of the abolitionists' "senseless and overbearing clamor."

The abolitionists, unfortunately, were skilled propagandists but reckless politicians. While Adams was still battering at the petition gag, they demanded other immediate challenges—a test vote, for example, on abolition in the District of Columbia. But Adams was too sharp a strategist to be pushed into political suicide. A test vote was "notoriously impracticable," he wrote on November 10, 1838. "There is in the present House of Representatives (a majority) of nearly two to one opposed to the consideration or discussion of the subject." A month later he insisted he could not collect five votes on such a test.

When the abolitionists kept bullying him, he complained that they "have already given me repeated warnings that they will desert and oppose me if I do not come over to *them* in the creed of *immediate* abolition."

If Adams fended them off politically, he warmly recognized the justice of their cause. "George Washington was abolitionist; so was Thomas Jefferson," he wrote the Rhode Island Anti-Slavery Society in 1838. "But were they alive, and should dare to show their faces and to utter the self-evident truth of the Declaration within the State of South Carolina, they would be hanged."

The election of the first Whig President, William Henry Harrison, in 1840 and Whig control of the House promised to bring the petition struggle to a climax. Opponents of the gag rule were picking up strength.

Organized in the spring of 1834, the Whigs were a hodgepodge of former National Republicans, anti-Jacksonites, states' rights men, and above all, the aristocracy of southern plantation owners who had been badly hurt by Jackson's removal of deposits from the United States Bank. Thus the South, already a dominant influence in the Democratic party, now largely controlled Whig policy as well. The alignment between northern and southern Whigs was dramatically evident in the gag votes, especially in 1837 when, without exception, all northern and southern Whigs supported the gag.

Southern dominance over the Army had prolonged the savage Seminole War in Florida, for troops had spent as much time hunting escaped slaves as they had fighting Indians. Southern influence in Washington had made a mockery of federal control over slave-running. Bitterly, Adams listed in his diary the key government offices filled by slaveholders in 1842—the President, President of the Senate, Speaker of the House, Chief Justice of the Supreme Court, commander in chief of the Army, and three of the six heads of executive departments.

Soon after Harrison's election, however, an antislavery coalition of insurgent Whig congressmen was formally organized for the first time. The chief spokesmen of this "Select Committee on Slavery," which established itself at Mrs. Sprigg's boarding house near the Capitol, were Joshua Giddings and Sherlock J. Andrews of Ohio, William Slade of Vermont, and Seth M. Gates of New York. Theodore Weld, a leading antislavery agitator, was sent to Washington to work with them, marking a new solidarity between abolitionists and moderates.

But it was Adams who dominated the group and kept its energies concentrated on the petition struggle. And it was Adams whom Whig leaders feared most, for his chairmanship of the House Committee on Foreign Affairs gave him a pivotal role in the dispute over the annexation of Texas.

The Whig leaders had decided that Adams must be destroyed once and for all. Whenever he rose on the House floor, they would badger him incessantly—as Weld reported to his wife, "screaming at the top of their voices: 'That is false.' 'I *demand* Mr. Speaker that you *put him down*.' 'I demand that you shut the mouth of that old harlequin.' 'What are we to sit here and endure such insults.'"

Adams fought back doggedly. "A perfect uproar like Babel would burst forth every two or three minutes as Mr. A. with his bold surgery would smite his cleaver into the very bones," Weld added. ". . . Mr. Adams would say, 'I see where the shoe pinches, Mr. Speaker, it will pinch *more* yet. I'll deal out to the gentlemen a diet that they'll find it hard to digest.'"

Adams finally gave the Whigs their long-sought opening—a petition from Haverhill, Massachusetts,

Gorsline

probably conceived by John Greenleaf Whittier, though not signed by him, praying for the peaceable dissolution of the Union. No petition so drastic had ever been introduced. Southern members rose in fury, demanding it be burned in the presence of the House. Henry A. Wise of Virginia called for censure, and Thomas F. Marshall of Kentucky, nephew of the Chief Justice, at once drafted the resolution of indictment. The crisis had come; Adams was fighting for his life.

At seventy-five, plagued by a hacking cough, pimples, and boils, Adams plunged eagerly into preparations for his defense. His energy was "astonishing," wrote Weld, who assisted him. "Last Friday, after he had been sitting in the house from 12 o'clock till 6, and for nearly half that time engaged in speaking with great energy against his ferocious assailants, I called at his house in the evening, and he came to me as fresh and elastic as a boy. I told him I was afraid he would tire himself out. 'No, no, not at all,' said he, 'I am all ready for another heat.' . . . He went on for an hour, or very nearly that, in a voice large enough to be heard by a large audience. Wonderful man!"

Adams had become a one-man symbol of the struggle against slavery. "One hundred members of the House represent slaves; four-fifths of whom would crucify me if their votes could erect the cross," he wrote in his diary. "Forty members, representatives of the free, in the league of slavery and mock Democracy, would break me on the wheel, if their votes or wishes could turn it round . . ."

Day after day, seemingly inexhaustible, Adams held the floor, his shrill voice slashing away at his enemies. Although he was literally a man without a party, new allies suddenly flocked to him. The tortuous petition struggle, and now the censure trial, at last captured the imagination of the North. News of the trial filled the headlines, most New England papers backing Adams. Petitions against censuring him poured into the House. His support reached far beyond the abolitionist groups now. At a mass meeting in Faneuil Hall on January 28, 1842, the leading men of Boston cheered his name and voted a resolution in his honor. At the most desperate moment in his life, Adams had actually reached the zenith of his power.

After two weeks of tumult on the House floor, the Whigs were tiring; even their leaders despaired of putting down Adams. Then, on February 7, he announced he would need a week more for his defense. The opposition completely crumbled. A motion to table the resolution of censure was quickly passed, 106 to 93. Still, Adams was not yet finished! He held the floor for the rest of the day, happily presenting two hundred petitions. Finally he went home, "scarcely

able to crawl up to my chamber," he wrote, "but with the sound of *Io triumphe* ringing in my ear."

The South recognized the significance of its defeat. Marshall, one of the prime movers of censure, went home to Kentucky, never to return to Congress. "The triumph of Mr. A. is complete," Weld wrote his wife. "This is the first victory over the slave holders *in a body* ever yet achieved since the foundation of the *government* and from this time their downfall *takes its date.*"

Adams was welcomed as a hero in Boston and Quincy. When he set out with his wife the next summer for a vacation through western New York, the trip unexpectedly became a festival of homage. In Buffalo there was a torchlight parade and an address by Millard Fillmore, who would himself ascend to the Presidency. In Syracuse and Utica, Adams was the guest of the city. When his train stopped for wood and water in Batavia, the whole town turned out. In Rochester he was greeted with booming cannon and ringing church bells.

Invited to Cincinnati to lay the cornerstone of the Astronomical Society, he was besieged by welcoming crowds as he passed through Ohio. At a reception in Akron, he was greeted with a kiss by the prettiest girl and noted happily, "I returned the salute on the lips, and kissed every woman that followed. . . ." At Covington, Kentucky, he recorded, "a very pretty woman . . . whispered, 'the first kiss in Kentucky'—which I did not refuse."

One slight setback marred an otherwise glorious year. Frustrated by Adams, the Whigs now took a small measure of revenge on his associate, Joshua Giddings. After a group of Virginia slaves on the ship *Creole* mutinied and escaped to Nassau,* Giddings introduced a resolution declaring they were not subject to Virginia law and thus had attained their natural freedom. For what the Whigs called a fiendish resolution, the House censured Giddings. He resigned his seat, went back to Ohio, and was promptly re-elected by a stunning majority.

Nothing, however, could halt Adams in the final stages of his triumph. The Democrats swept the nation in the fall of 1843, taking control of the House. The gag rule could muster only a slim majority of three votes. "The truth is that the slaveholders got so smitten with consternation at the bolts of father Adams hurled through the ranks at their last session," Weld proclaimed, "that they have never been able to rally."

At the opening of the new session in December,

* When a group of Negro mutineers seized the slave ship *Amistad* in 1839, they were successfully defended by Adams before the Supreme Court (*see* "The Slave Ship Rebellion," AMERICAN HERITAGE, February, 1957).

1844, Adams was convinced he had enough votes for a final showdown. After eight years under the restraining bonds of the gag rule, he confidently submitted a motion to rescind it. The motion was passed that very day, 105 to 80.

It was the most spectacular battle any congressman had ever waged, and for most of the eight years Adams had stood alone. He had opened the halls of Congress to the slavery debate, taken it from the narrow arena of the abolitionists and forced it into the very fulcrum of national politics. Younger men like Giddings would continue to press the attack in Congress, and on a state and local level, the Liberty party had already made slavery the crucial political issue. "Blessed, ever blessed be the name of God," Adams wrote in his diary that night.

Although shrewd realism kept him from complete alignment with the abolitionists, he had made himself the dominant figure of the antislavery movement. As early as 1839, he had submitted three radical resolutions to the House. The first set July 4, 1842, as the date after which any child born to slave parents would be declared free. The second prohibited any future slave states except Florida. The third declared slavery and the slave trade illegal in the District of Columbia after July 4, 1845. It was an eminently practical plan of gradual abolition, but the House ignored it. With its defeat probably disappeared one of the last comprehensive chances for a peaceful settlement of the mounting crisis over slavery.

On the morning of November 20, 1846, after rising as usual before five o'clock and breakfasting with his family, Adams took a brisk walk to the new Harvard Medical College. On the way, he was stricken with what was probably a light cerebral hemorrhage. Yet his recovery was remarkably quick. In a few months he was riding around Boston in his carriage. When he returned to his seat in Congress, sectional differences were momentarily forgotten. The whole House, North and South alike, stood as one man. "Old Man Eloquent," the nation's last great link with its Revolutionary heritage, was back.

On Monday, February 21, 1848, Adams, now eighty-one, reached the House early. President Polk had just received the treaty of peace with Mexico. A roll call was going on, and the House was filled with clatter. Suddenly a member seated nearby Adams saw the old man's face redden, while his right hand clutched at the corner of his desk. Then he slumped over.

Someone cried out and caught Adams in his arms. They carried him to the cleared area in front of the Speaker's table, where he was placed on a sofa and moved to the Speaker's room. Henry Clay stood by,

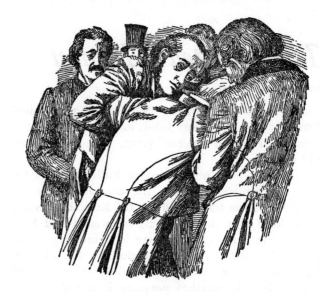

weeping. For a few minutes Adams revived. Leaning close, John Palfrey, the former Unitarian clergyman and Harvard professor, now a staunch antislavery congressman, heard him say, "This is the end of earth, but I am composed."

His wife, Louisa, arrived, but Adams, half paralyzed, had lapsed into a coma and gave no sign of recognition. He lingered through Washington's Birthday and at 7:20 on the evening of February 23 passed away.

The service three days later was probably the greatest public tribute since Franklin had been buried in Philadelphia. Thousands of people had filed by his coffin while he lay in state in the House; southern leaders joined the North in homage. "Where could death have found him but at the post of duty," proclaimed Senator Thomas Hart Benton. That morning, a cannon salute started at sunrise and continued during the funeral procession. Then the body was taken to Faneuil Hall in Boston, where thousands more paid homage, and over the entrance they placed the inscription: "Born a citizen of Massachusetts. Died a citizen of the United States."

He was buried in Quincy in the old family tomb in the churchyard. At the last moment a southern congressman in the funeral party stepped forward and, stooping before the Adams vault, called out, "Good bye, Old Man!"

In addition to The Bold Brahmins, *a study of the antislavery movement in New England, Lawrence Lader is the author of* The Margaret Sanger Story. *His account of the 1863 draft riots, "New York's Bloodiest Week," appeared in the June, 1959, issue of* AMERICAN HERITAGE.

For further reading: The Anti-slavery Impulse, *by G. H. Barnes (Appleton-Century, 1933);* John Quincy Adams and the Union, *by Samuel F. Bemis (Knopf, 1956);* Crusade Against Slavery, *by Louis Filler (Harper, 1960).*

The Wasted Mission

CONTINUED FROM PAGE 45

communication, but if the President of the United States had attached any value to it he would have brought it before the conference, and he certainly did not."

Wilson, indeed, never brought Bullitt's report before the conference; quite the contrary, when he turned his "one track mind" to the Russian question he ordered that the report be suppressed and kept secret. The newspapermen were left clutching at rumors. Though many projects tended to suffer a lingering death at the Hotel Crillon, Bullitt's succumbed swiftly: for all practical purposes it was dead and abandoned within forty-eight hours after Bullitt's return to Paris. It was replaced by a plan to supply Russia with food upon the conditions that all hostilities cease and that the Russian railroads be placed under the supervision of a relief commission. Early in May, the Soviet government turned the offer down, protesting that the true objectives of the plan were not humanitarian but political, and demanding instead full-fledged peace negotiations. That demand was to be ignored by the United States for fourteen years.

Why Wilson disregarded the Bullitt report is the mystery within the fantasy. Perhaps only a mind reader could tell with confidence what the increasingly secretive President was thinking. Bullitt himself has suggested at least two theories. On the one hand he has said that his report was abandoned because, at the moment of his return to Paris, the White armies had made substantial advances, and it was hoped that the Soviet government might soon be destroyed by force of arms. But Wilson did not share that hope. Trying to stop Bolshevism with an army, he said on March 27, was like using a broom to stop the sea. Somewhat petulantly, Bullitt has also suggested that when Wilson found out that Bullitt had gone first to see Lloyd George, he took it as a personal affront and refused to see Bullitt out of sheer pique.

A somewhat more substantial explanation of Wilson's behavior can be suggested. From the very start of the conference it had been recognized that there were really only three possible policies toward Russia. First, an all-out effort to crush the still-weak Soviet regime by force of arms. Churchill advocated this, but Wilson would not hear of it; even if the American public would accept further military activity (which it would not), the idea was repugnant to Wilson personally. He had been reluctant enough to go to war against the Kaiser; he could not attack a regime which

at least purported to be a manifestation of popular will and a revolt against despotism.

In 1917 Wilson had looked with the warmest sympathy upon the March revolution in Russia. Coming as it did only weeks before America's entry into the war, it had removed "the one objection to affirming that the European war was a war between Democracy and Absolutism . . ."—or so the Secretary of State had advised. America had been the first country to recognize the Provisional government led so briefly by Alexander Kerensky. It was hard now for Wilson to believe that what had once seemed so promising a beginning had passed irretrievably from the scene. In any event, the President felt that a peace conference which was, uniquely, to rest upon the collective will of mankind could not start out by crushing the Russian revolution.

A second alternative was the *cordon sanitaire*—encircling Soviet Russia with hostile countries in order to contain the Bolshevik plague. Clemenceau strongly urged this, but Wilson again demurred. *Cordon sanitaire* was a euphemism for a holy alliance and the re-creation of a balance of power, and that, Wilson thought, had been a major cause of the World War. America, he had said, would join no alliance that was not an alliance of all countries.

The third alternative—urged by Bullitt and, occasionally, Lloyd George—was to recognize the Soviet regime as a *de facto* government. Still Wilson could not go along. He had long believed that recognition should be extended only to regimes which bore the hallmarks of constitutional legitimacy. The Bolsheviks had not only seized power by force, they had forcefully disbanded the popularly elected Constituent Assembly. Moreover, it was difficult to see how a regime dedicated to world revolution could be "a fit partner for a league of honor." The very language of Soviet diplomacy, even when suing for peace and conciliation, seemed calculated to antagonize and exacerbate. Wilson described it as "studiously insulting." Weak and disorganized though Soviet Russia was, her ministers addressed the West in terms of hostility and contempt. On October 24, 1918, for example, Foreign Minister Chicherin had written the President:

. . . Even though your Government has not yet been replaced by a Council of People's Commissars and your post is not yet taken by Eugene Debs, whom you have imprisoned . . . just as we have concluded peace with the imperialist government of Germany, with Emperor Wilhelm at its head, whom you, Mr. President, hold in no greater esteem than we . . . hold you, we finally propose to you, Mr. President, that you take up with your Allies the following questions and give us precise and business-like replies: Do the Governments of the United States, England, and France intend to cease demanding the blood of the Russian people . . . if the Russian people will agree to pay them a ransom . . . ? If so, just what tribute do [you] demand . . . ?

This letter, and others in the same vein, hardly served to suggest that Soviet Russia was eager to become a law-abiding, self-restrained, coequal member of the society of nations. True, Wilson told a reporter that "if I thought that . . . any clause or phrase [of the League Covenant] forbade to any peoples the sacred right of revolution, I would tear up the Covenant with my own hands." But the President really hoped that by reforming the world the League would outflank world revolution.

Unwilling to acknowledge that Soviet autocracy had become part of the scheme of things, Wilson was waiting for some sign of change, some sign that the revolution was settling down into tractable, constitutional, parliamentary patterns. He was willing to encourage such a change. "I visualize it like this," he told William Wiseman in October, 1918. "A lot of impossible folk, fighting among themselves. You cannot do business with them, so you shut them off up in a room and lock the door and tell them that when they have settled matters among themselves you will unlock the door and do business."

This of course had been the idea behind the Prinkipo proposal. If all the factions could be gotten together and persuaded to lay their cards on the table, they might contrive to constitutionalize themselves. One can see in Wilson's mind a picture of Bolsheviks and Monarchists sitting opposite each other in long rows like so many Whigs and Tories—with Mensheviks and Social Revolutionists somewhere in the back benches. And a Lenin somehow transmuted into the leader of the loyal majority Wilson would gladly deal with—however radical the man's economics might be.

Nor was this view, in retrospect so naïve, an aberration peculiar to Wilson. The best informed among his advisers suggested much the same view. Shortly before the armistice, Walter Lippmann and Frank Cobb advised that "the Peace Conference might well send a message asking for the creation of a government sufficiently representative to speak for [the Russian] territories." Persuaded, as were most Americans in 1919, that parliamentary, constitutional democracy was the wave of the future, Wilson was prepared to wait if need be for things to settle down. In May he said that he no longer regretted not having a Russian policy; under present conditions it was impossible to define one.

But William C. Bullitt was a young man, and impatient. He was bitterly disappointed with the abandonment of his project, and when in May he saw the text of the Treaty of Versailles, he gave up in despair. On May 17 he submitted his resignation to the Secretary of State. He submitted, too, a stinging letter to the President, in which he said that the grounds had been laid for another century of war. "Russia, 'the acid test of good will,' for me as for you, has not even been understood . . ." he wrote. "I am sorry that you did not fight our fight to the finish and that you had so little faith in the millions of men, like myself, in every nation who had faith in you." And with a keen sense of the dramatic, he told the press that he was going to lie on the sands of the Riviera and watch the world go to hell.

On June 28, the peace treaty was signed at Versailles, and the men at the Hotel Crillon packed their bags. Six months after it opened, the peace conference had adjourned, the Allies separating with the announcement that they had made perpetual peace. Siberia and Russia were still at war.

Bullitt had not quite made *his* peace. From Paris he retired not to the Riviera but to the Maine woods, from whence he was summoned in August by the Senate Committee on Foreign Relations. Appearing before the committee on Friday morning, September 12, he was not a reluctant witness; "he simply turned state's evidence," Senator Henry Cabot Lodge later said. To the amazement and delight of the senators and the acute embarrassment of his former colleagues and superiors, Bullitt told the full story of his "secret" trip to Moscow; he described his breakfast with Lloyd George, the terms that House and Kerr had given him, his conversations with Chicherin and Lenin, and Wilson's decision to suppress his report. Having polished off his Russian mission, Bullitt went on to report that all of Wilson's chief advisers had privately expressed their disapproval of the Treaty of Versailles. He brought laughter to the lips of the senators when he quoted Lansing as saying that the Senate would vote against the treaty if only they could understand it.

Wilson was in the midst of his great tour of the West, speaking for the treaty, when the news of Bullitt's testimony reached him. Two weeks later he suffered the stroke that ended the tour. When Wilson recovered, he accepted Lansing's resignation; the Bullitt affair had been a climactic skirmish in the long battle between the President and his Secretary of State.

In November, as if to expunge an ugly memory, two of the former American peace commissioners at Paris wrote the secretary general of the American Commission to Negotiate the Peace that they could find no record "official or otherwise" which authorized the credentials that Bullitt had been given in February. "We, the undersigned," they concluded, "desire now to make of record in the archives of the American Peace Delegation the fact that at no time was the mission of Mr. Bullitt discussed—much less acted upon—in our presence, either at any meeting of the American Delegation or elsewhere . . ."

Thus was concluded the fantasy which had begun as America's first diplomatic contact with Soviet Russia. The Soviet had purported to be willing to forswear the bulk of the historically Russian territories. The Allies had said, in effect, that they had not heard about it. The situation was anomalous, if not comical. It was, of course, only the first act. (The second contained an element of poetic justice: In 1933 William Bullitt went to Moscow once again, this time as the first American Ambassador to the U.S.S.R. He stayed until 1936, by which time the Stalin purges were getting under way.) Yet for all its absurdity, the Bullitt mission posed the dilemma that in the ensuing four decades has gradually become the major theme of world diplomacy:

Could the democracies afford to do business with Soviet Russia?

Could they afford not to?

A student at Harvard Law School, Robert S. Rifkind is the author of a previous article in American Heritage, *"The Colonel's Dream of Power," a study of Edward House's little-remembered venture into fiction, Philip Dru.*

The Johnson County War

CONTINUED FROM PAGE 53

blizzards in memory. They plodded along without speaking, while beards and mustaches became coated with ice, and the wind lashed knife-edged snow in their faces. Halting before daybreak to thaw out around sagebrush fires, they went on until they looked down over a low bluff at the still-sleeping KC ranch.

Two innocent visitors, trappers, had been spending the night in the cabin. As first one and then the other sauntered forth into the gray morning air, he was recognized as not among the wanted men, and as soon as a corner of the barn hid him from the house, each was made prisoner. After a long wait Champion's friend Nick Ray finally appeared and was shot down. The door opened, and Champion himself faced a storm of bullets to drag Ray inside.

The fusillade went on for hour after hour. In the log shack Nate Champion was writing, with a cramped hand in a pocket notebook, the record of his last hours.

Me and Nick was getting breakfast when the attack took place. Two men was with us—Bill Jones and another man. The old man went after water and did not come back. His friend went to see what was the matter and he did not come back. Nick started out and I told him to look out, that I thought there was someone at the stable and would not let them come back.

Nick is shot but not dead yet. He is awful sick. I must go and wait on him.

It is now about two hours since the first shot. Nick is still alive.

They are still shooting and are all around the house, Boys, there is bullets coming in here like hail.

Them fellows is in such shape I can't get at them. They are shooting from the stable and river and back of the house.

Nick is dead. He died about 9 o'clock.

Hour after hour the hills crackled with rifle fire, and such was the emptiness of the country that while the besiegers were on a main road, such as it was, connecting civilization with a little settlement at the back of beyond, they could bang away all day without fear of interruption. Or almost. As it happened there was a slight interruption in midafternoon.

Jack Flagg, a rustler intellectual of sorts, had left his ranch eighteen miles up the Red Fork of Powder River on this snowy morning of April 9, on his way to the Democratic state convention at Douglas, to which he was a delegate from Johnson County. It was one of the oddities of the situation that the thieves were all Democrats, and the murderers were all Republicans. A rancher, newspaper editor, and schoolteacher, Flagg was an accomplished demagogue who had twisted the tails of the big outfits by means fair and foul. He was very much on the wanted list.

He was riding about fifty yards or so behind a wagon driven by his seventeen-year-old stepson; and since the invaders had withdrawn into a strategy huddle and pulled in their pickets, there was no sound of firing to warn him as the wagon rattled downhill to the bridge by the KC. Flagg started over to the house to greet his friends, and was ordered to halt by someone who failed to recognize him.

"Don't shoot me, boys, I'm all right," he called gaily, taking it for a joke. Under the hail of bullets which disabused him, he fled back to the wagon and slashed the tugs holding one of the team, and he and the boy made their miraculous escape.

The wagon Flagg left behind was put to use by the invaders. Since hours of cannonading had failed to dislodge Champion, they loaded it with old hay and dry chips and pushed it up to the cabin, where they set it afire. Flames and smoke rolled skyward until they wondered if the man inside had cheated them by shooting himself. Champion, however, was still writing.

I heard them splitting wood. I guess they are going to fire the house to-night.
I think I will make a break when night comes if alive.
It's not night yet.
The house is all fired. Goodbye boys, if I never see you again.

Nathan D. Champion.

Finally, he broke through the roof at one end of the house and sprinted desperately for the cover of a little draw, which he never reached.

Pawing over the body, the invaders found and read the diary, after which it was presented to the Chicago newsman. Its contents survived, to become a classic of raw courage in the annals of the West.

Next day, Sunday, April 10, the invaders were approaching Buffalo when they were met by a rider on a lathered horse, who warned them that the town was in an uproar and they had better turn back if they

valued their lives. They had just made a rest halt at the friendly TA ranch. Their only hope was to return there and dig in.

Sam Clover, ace reporter, was too smart for that trap. Deciding to take his chance with the aroused local population, he left the now deflated avengers and rode on into Buffalo, where he did some fast talking and finally got himself under the wing of his old friend Major Edmond G. Fechet of the 6th Cavalry, with whom he had campaigned during the Ghost Dance troubles in North Dakota. With the rest of the 6th, Fechet was now stationed at Fort McKinney, near Buffalo. So Clover rode off to the fort to luxuriate in hot baths and clean sheets and to write dispatches, while the wretched invaders prepared to stand siege for their lives.

They worked all night, and by morning of the eleventh were entrenched behind a very efficient set of fortifications at the TA ranch, where they were virtually impregnable except for a shortage of food supplies. By morning they were besieged by an impromptu army of hornet-mad cowboys and ranchmen, led by Sheriff "Red" Angus of Johnson County. The army numbered over three hundred on the day of surrender.

In Buffalo, churches and schools were turned into headquarters for the steadily arriving recruits; ladies baked cakes to send to Sheriff Angus' command post; the young Methodist preacher, who was possessed of no mean tongue, employed it to denounce this crime of the century. The leading merchant, a venerable Scotsman named Robert Foote, mounted his black horse and, with his long white beard flying in the breeze, dashed up and down the streets, calling the citizens to arms. More impressive still, he threw open his store, inviting them to help themselves to ammunition, slickers, blankets, flour—everything. He was said to be a heavy dealer in rustled beef, and on the invaders' list; but so was almost everyone of importance in Buffalo.

The telegraph wires had been cut repeatedly since the start of the invasion, but on April 12 they were working again momentarily, and a friend in Buffalo got a telegram through to the governor with the first definite word of the invaders' plight. From that time on, all the heavy artillery of influence, from Cheyenne to Washington and on up to the White House, was brought to bear to rescue the cattlemen from the consequences of their act.

Senators Carey and Warren called at the executive mansion late that night and got President Benjamin Harrison out of bed. He was urged to suppress an insurrection in Wyoming, though the question of just who was in insurrection against whom was not clarified. Telegrams flew back and forth. At 12:50 A.M. on April 13, Colonel J. J. Van Horn of the 6th Cavalry wired the commanding general of the Department of the Platte, acknowledging receipt of orders to proceed to the TA ranch.

Two hours later, three troops of the 6th filed out of Fort McKinney in the freezing dark, in a thoroughly disgusted frame of mind because (a) they had just come in that afternoon from chasing a band of marauding Crows back to the reservation and did not relish being ordered out again at three in the morning; and furthermore because (b) they were heartily on the side of Johnson County and would rather have left the invaders to their fate.

© THE LEADER CO.

They reached the TA at daybreak. Inside the beleaguered ranch house Major Wolcott and his men, their food exhausted, were preparing to make a break as soon as it was sufficiently light. They had eaten what they thought would be their last breakfast, and were awaiting the lookout's whistle which would call them to make that last desperate run—like so many Nate Champions—into the ring of hopelessly outnumbering rifles.

But hark! Instead of the suicide signal, a cavalry bugle! Major Wolcott crossed to a window.

"Gentlemen, it is the troops!"

From start to finish the Johnson County story reads like a parody of every Hollywood western ever filmed, and never more so than at this moment. Down the hill swept a line of seven horsemen abreast; between the fluttering pennons rode Colonel Van Horn, Major Fechet, Sheriff Angus; a representative of the governor, who would not have stuck his neck into northern Wyoming at this point for anything; and, of course, Sam T. Clover of the Chicago *Herald*. One of the guidon bearers carried a white handkerchief. An answering flutter of white appeared on the breastworks. Major Wolcott advanced stiffly and saluted Colonel Van Horn.

"I will surrender to you, but to that man"—indicating Sheriff Angus—"never!"

Forty-four prisoners were marched off to the fort, not including the few defectors and two of the Texas mercenaries, who later died of wounds. Of the ringleaders, only one had received so much as a scratch.

"The cattlemen's war" was front-paged all over the nation for some three weeks, with the Boston *Transcript* putting tongue in cheek to remark on the ever-widening activities of Harvard men. Then the rest of the country forgot it. Four days after the surrender, still guarded by unsympathetic troops, the prisoners were removed to Fort Russell, near Cheyenne. Here they were safely away from Johnson County, which had, however, been behaving with remarkable restraint. The weather was worse than ever and the march overland one of the most miserable on record. Apart from that, the killers got off at no heavier cost to themselves than minor inconvenience and some ignominy. They were never brought to justice.

They did, however, pay an admitted $100,000 as the price of the invasion, counting legal expenses and not mentioning the illegal. Of the sordid features of the Johnson County invasion which all but defy comment, the worst was the affair of the trappers. These two simple and unheroic men, who had been with Champion and Nick Ray in the cabin and had the bad luck to witness the KC slaughter, were hustled out of the state under an escort of gunmen in terror of their lives, and thence across Nebraska to Omaha, where they were piled onto a train, still under escort of gunmen and lawyers, and delivered at an eastern destination. The Johnson County authorities and their friends had been trying frantically to get them back, but no subpoenas could be issued because the cattlemen, still protected by the army, were not yet formally charged with anything. Counting bribes to federal officers and judges, legal fees, forfeited bail, and other expenses, it was said to have cost

$27,000 to get the witnesses across Nebraska alone. The trappers had been promised a payoff of $2,500 each, and given postdated checks. When presented for cashing, the checks proved to be on a bank that had never existed.

Meanwhile the armor of self-pity remained undented. In their own eyes and those of their friends, the cattlemen were the innocent victims of an outrage. While awaiting a hearing at Fort Russell, they were kept in the lightest of durance, coming and going freely to Cheyenne. Major Wolcott was permitted a trip outside the state. When Fred DeBillier showed signs of cracking under the strain of captivity, raving and uttering strange outcries in the middle of the night, he was tenderly removed, first to a hotel and later to his home in New York, for rest and medical treatment.

Eventually the prisoners were transferred to the state penitentiary at Laramie, where the district judge who ordered the removal assured Governor Amos W. Barber that these important persons would by no means be required to mingle with ordinary convicts. They were then escorted to their new quarters by a guard of honor, which included Wyoming's adjutant general and acting secretary of state.

Public opinion was overwhelmingly against the prisoners, but it was poorly led and ineffective, and public wrath was dissipated into thin air. On their side, however, in the words of a newspaper correspondent, the cattlemen were "backed not only by the Republican machine from President Harrison on down to the state organization, but by at least twenty-five million dollars in invested capital. They have the President, the governor, the courts, their United States Senators, the state legislature and the army at their backs." It was enough.

One sequel to the episode was an attempt to muzzle the press. A small-town editor who criticized the cattlemen too violently was jailed on a charge of criminal libel and held for thirty days—long enough to silence his paper. A second editor was beaten. But the latter, whose name was A. S. Mercer, exacted an eye for an eye in his celebrated chronicle of the invasion, published two years later and resoundingly entitled: *The Banditti of the Plains, or The Cattlemen's Invasion of Wyoming. The Crowning Infamy of the Ages.*

Thereupon his print shop was burned to the ground, and another subservient judge ordered all copies of the book seized and burned. But while they were awaiting the bonfire, a wagonload of them was removed one night and drawn by galloping horses over the Colorado line. Thereafter copies on library shelves were stolen and mutilated as far away as the Library of Congress until only a few were left. But two new editions have since been published, and so—in the end—Mr. Mercer won.

The same judge who had shown himself so solicitous of the prisoners' comfort granted a change of venue from Johnson County, not to a neutral county but to the cattlemen's own stronghold in Cheyenne. The trial was set for January 2, 1893. Nineteen days later over a thousand veniremen had been examined and there were still only eleven men on the jury. The prolonged financial strain was too much for Johnson County; since there were no witnesses anyway, the prosecution tossed in the towel, and the case was dismissed.

The so-called rustlers came out with the cleaner hands. Good luck had saved them from spilling the blood of the invaders; and while there was one unsolved killing of a cattlemen's adherent afterward, this appears to have been an act of personal grudge, not of community vengeance. The chain reaction of retaliatory murders that could have started never did; and strife-torn Johnson County settled down to peace. The roundups became democratic, with big and little stockmen working side by side. Montagu sons married Capulet daughters; notorious rustlers turned into respectable ranchmen and hobnobbed with their former enemies. One was mentioned for governor, and another rose to high position in—of all things—the Wyoming Stock Growers Association.

Yet, if bitterness has mercifully subsided, a certain remnant of injustice remains. The ghosts of old wrongs unrighted still walk in Buffalo, and, with the law cheated of its due, the pleasant little town with its creek and its cottonwood trees can only wait for that earthly equivalent of the Last Judgment, the verdict of history.

Helena Huntington Smith, of Alexandria, Virginia, has written several books and articles about the West. Her previous articles for AMERICAN HERITAGE *have included "Pioneers in Petticoats" (February, 1959) and "A Few Men in Soldier Suits" (August, 1957).*

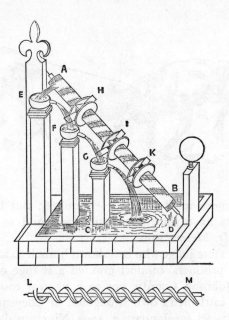

1. This is one of the oldest of schemes. Proprietors of water mills—particularly those on streams that dried up periodically—frequently came up with this plan. The idea, based upon the Archimedean screw, struck with such blinding force that the inventor could only shout "Eureka!" The bottom diagram, L to M, shows an Archimedean screw. It is built into the hollow tube, A to B. Water flows successively from the overflow spouts of basins E, F, and G, striking waterwheels H, I, and K to turn the Archimedean screw. The screw, in turn, carries the water up from reservoir C-D to the top basin again. Perpetual motion! Why won't it work?

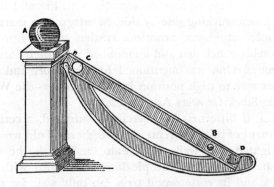

2. Like all great ideas, this one is magnificently simple. Atop the pedestal, at A, is a powerful "lodestone," or magnet. It attracts iron ball B up the track. Near the top of the track the ball falls through hole C, rolls along the curved bottom track and out through the one-way door at D. Up she goes again. Makes you a little tired to watch it. The ball, says the inventor, will keep rolling forever. This one is bound to work. Or is it?

Why won't

The search for perpetual
of obsessed inventors, an

By CLIFFORD

The idea of perpetual motion—something for nothing under the laws of physics—is as insidious as any in history. It will not lie down and die. To this day, the persistence of the idea is the one thing perpetual about it. The Patent Office is still pestered by single-minded inventors of "self-motors," the technical section of the Library of Congress is haunted by furtive figures, and editors of scientific magazines regularly receive correspondence from dreamers with "new" plans for solving the most famous scientific problem of all time.

Over the decades, indeed centuries, each inventor of this sort seems to have lived sealed off from the rest of the world, working in the perfect vacuum that he so avidly desired to make his contraption spin forever. Everything has been tried—overbalanced wheels, rolling weights, water wheels endlessly pumping their own water, inclined planes, squirrel cages with steel squirrels forever pursuing a magnet, even rings of balloons inflating under water, hopefully *ad infinitum*, to lift themselves to the surface.

In time perpetual motion became a true scientific puzzle, with set rules. The device, once completed, had to move and continue forever (or until the parts wore out) without any assistance except from gravity, buoyancy, or magnetism. This immediately ruled out all schemes to use the daily variations in temperature and air pressure or the constant motion of waves and tides. If the machine could do useful work, so much the better, but the machine did not have to be useful—it just had to keep going.

The first efforts at perpetual motion in this country probably predated the Revolution, but the idea had been born in some fertile brain long before. It is believed that Leonardo da Vinci dallied with it. The first printed reference to the problem occurs in 1579, and the earliest British patent for a perpetual-motion machine was granted March 9, 1635. Then, between 1855 and 1903, nearly six hundred applications were made to the British Patent Office.

they work?

motion is a tragicomedy

eager faith, and humbug

B. HICKS

The obsession leaped the Atlantic and found a fertile field in the United States. An unknown number of perpetual-motion patents (believed to be about ten) were granted and on file in the Patent Office when the building burned in 1836. Letters of patent continued to be granted until it became apparent that perpetual motion was an illusion.

As early as 1828 the journal of the Franklin Institute carried a long explanation of why "perpetual motion" could not be perpetual. When they accepted the principle of the conservation of energy, propounded around 1850 by Joule and others, scientists as a whole tacitly denied the possibility of a *perpetuum mobile,* and at last the government took the stand, which it maintains to this day, that an application for a perpetual-motion patent must include a working model.

But once the notion had fired a man's brain, he could not be convinced that perpetual motion was impossible. American inventors simply ignored the discouraging statements of scientists. Their heyday, which stretched from about 1825 to 1910, was a period of optimism, when many long-sought goals were attained. Steam performed new wonders, sewing machines made

Buried in every perpetual-motion scheme is a flaw in the inventor's reasoning. Frequently the basic idea is so clever that even a trained observer has difficulty in peeling away the layers of brilliant logic and unearthing that fatal error. Nor is it usually the simple argument that there is "too much friction." The author's simplified diagrams show some of the classic perpetual-motion schemes which Americans have invented and reinvented scores of times. In each of the schemes a law of nature, a basic principle which the inventor has overlooked, is going to stop the device. With each machine, the inventor's claims are given. What is wrong? The correct answers are on page 85.

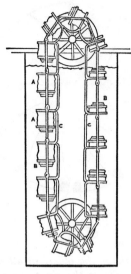

3. This rig operates mostly in water. All of the bellows (A) are interconnected by hollow tubes (C). As each bellows starts up the left side of the rig, a weight (B) pulls it open. On the right side of the rig, the weight closes the bellows. There is more air on the left side than on the right. Air is lighter than water. This one is bound to operate. No?

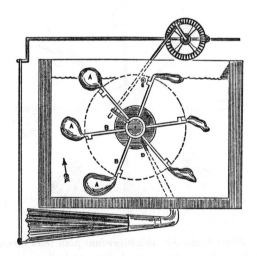

4. If gravity won't work, buoyancy will. The drawing shows a tank of water. Inside the tank is a wheel, and around the wheel are bags or bladders (A), installed on hollow tubes (B). Below the tank is a bellows operated by a crank attached to the wheel. It is obvious that the inflated bags on the left will cause the wheel to turn in a clockwise direction. At point E they pass a valve that deflates them, and at point D they pass another valve which inflates them with a mighty blast from the bellows, which meanwhile is being operated by the crank as the wheel turns. True, the machine doesn't look like much, but it works like fury. Why shouldn't it?

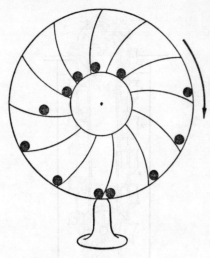

5. *This is perhaps the oldest of all overbalanced wheels. The balls at the right are obviously farther from the pivot point than those at the left, so the wheel will spin clockwise until you get so tired of listening to the balls roll that you put it in a far corner of the attic. What will stop it?*

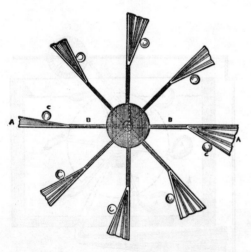

6. *There is more to this ingenious plan than meets the eye. The arms (B) are hollow, and all are interconnected at the hub. Each arm terminates in a bellows (A). Heavy balls (C) open and close the bellows by gravity. The air is removed from the system, which then is filled with mercury. As one of the arms reaches a horizontal position at the left, the weight of the ball closes the bellows, forcing out the mercury. Meanwhile the opposite bellows, on the right, is being opened by the weight of its ball, and receives the load of mercury. Obviously there is always more weight of mercury on the right side of the wheel than on the left. Ergo, it will spin forever. Or have we possibly overlooked something?*

stitches, carriages ran without horses, and airplanes flew like birds. These marvels achieved, what layman would doubt that water could eventually be made to run uphill by itself, or that a wheel could be designed to be constantly heavier on one side than on the other and so spin forever? Newspapers were believers, too; the Philadelphia *Gazette* reported in 1829:

We were much gratified yesterday with the result of an examination of a self-moving machine, which may be seen at Bowlsby's Merchants' Hotel, in Slater Street, and which the inventor calls perpetual motion. We have no doubt of it being nearer a perpetual self-moving principle than any invention which has preceded it, and as near as any we shall ever see. The great merit, aside from its practical uses, is its simplicity, and the certainty and readiness with which you perceive that it covers no trick or deception.

Anyone, including editors, who believed in a particular device seems to have clung to his belief with the tenacity of the inventor himself. A shining example of such loyalty appeared in the New York *Journal of Commerce*, which in 1854 described a machine invented by one J. G. Hendrickson:

The model was in our office yesterday, and attached to some clockwork, which it turned without once stopping to breathe. We see no reason why it should not go until worn out! After a careful examination, we can safely say, in all seriousness, that the propelling power is self-contained and self-adjusting, and gives sufficient force to carry ordinary clockwork, and all without any winding up or replenishing.

In 1868, the *Journal* published a follow-up:

About fourteen years ago we published the first description of a machine invented by Mr. James G. Hendrickson of Freehold, N.J. . . . [and] we saw no reason why it would not go until it was worn out. The inventor was an old man, who had spent his whole life in pursuit of the object he had now attained. He was invited to be present at various fairs and exhibitions of new inventions, and wherever he went, his machine formed one of the chief attractions. The professors were all against him. Accordingly, Mr. H. was seized at Keyport, N.J., for practising "jugglery" under the "Act for Suppressing Vice and Immorality." To expose the supposed trick, an axe was brought, and the cylinder splintered into fragments. Alas! There was no concealed spring, and the machine had "gone of itself." He made a new machine. His model once more completed, was constructed of brass, hollow throughout. The moment the blocks were taken out, the wheels started off "like a thing of life"; and, during ten months, it never once stopped. The inventor had perfected two new machines, and made a very comfortable livelihood exhibiting them, prosecuting his efforts meanwhile to secure his patent. Age crept upon him, however, before this point was reached; and last Saturday afternoon he breathed his last at Freehold. The night after his death his shop was broken open, and both models stolen. (!)

Here was a field made to order for fakers, and all kinds of humbugs were built to fleece a gullible public. Perhaps the most notable of these devices, and certainly the most fascinating, was the Redheffer perpetual-motion machine, described many years later by Daniel Hering. It was twice exposed, once by a pair of trained eyes, and again by a pair of sensitive and famous ears.

Charles Redheffer (or Redhoeffer) first appeared with his marvelous machine in Philadelphia in 1812. He installed it in a home on the city's outskirts, charging admission to watch it run, seemingly as long as he wished. Soon Philadelphia became embroiled in an argument as to whether this really was the long-sought perpetual motion. Huge wagers were made as to its authenticity. Charles Gobert, a civil engineer (perhaps in the pay of Redheffer), placed the following announcement in the Philadelphia *Gazette*, July 12, 1813:

I hereby offer, on demand, any bet or bets from 6,000 to 100,000 dollars, to the end of proving, in a few days, both by mathematical data and three several experiments, to the satisfaction of enlightened judges, chosen by my very opponents out of the most respectable gentlemen of this city, or of New York, that Mr. Redheffer's discovery is genuine, and that it is incontestibly a perpetual self-moving principle . . . This is to be valid until the 15th inst., at sunsetting.

At this juncture, the Pennsylvania legislature took an interest and appointed a commission of eminent engineers to decide upon the validity of Redheffer's machine, probably the only time in American history that a perpetual-motion machine was so dignified.

On the appointed day the commission appeared at the house and found it locked. No one answered the bell. However, through a barred window the commissioners could see the machine working in lonely magnificence. It consisted of weighted cars continually ascending and descending inclined planes. A shaft was geared to it, apparently to perform useful work.

One of the commissioners, Nathan Sellers, had brought along his son, Coleman, reputed to be a mechanical genius. Peering through the window, young Sellers noticed something which escaped the attention of the adults. At the point where the shaft was geared to the mechanism, the cogged wheels were a bit worn, and they were worn *on the wrong side of the cogs.* Only one conclusion was possible: instead of *powering* the shaft, the mechanism was *powered by* the shaft.

When the lad told his father what he had seen, the senior Sellers hired a skilled mechanic to make a machine identical to Redheffer's, except that it was driven by a spring concealed in an ornamental post (a device that was to become a favorite of later fakers). Redheffer, brought to see the machine, was thunderstruck.

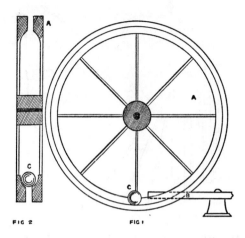

7. An inventor, his brain afire with perpetual motion, once watched a squirrel running endlessly in a squirrel cage. At last! Here was the answer! Figure 1 shows a wheel (A) and Figure 2 the same wheel in cross section. As the drawings indicate, the wheel is formed in two sections upon one shaft, with an opening between the halves. C is an iron ball, and B is a strong magnet projecting between the halves of the wheel. The magnet continually attracts the ball up the inclined side of the wheel, but its weight causes the wheel to turn. The ball stays where it is, the wheel goes round and round. If a squirrel can do it, why can't this rig?

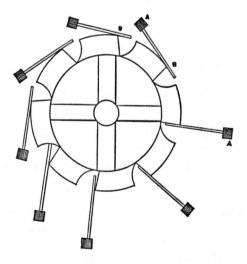

8. Here is a simple variation of the overbalanced wheel that even a child can build to enjoy in his old age. Weighted arms (A) are pivoted at points B. As the wheel moves, they fall into their extended positions, overbalancing the wheel and causing it to spin forever. Are there any questions from the class?

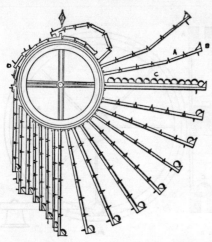

9. *Magnificent, isn't it? This creation has twenty-one arms to pull itself into the dim, dim future. Each of the arms (A) is built in hinged sections, which become rigid as they flop over to the right. At the end of each arm is a cup (B). C is a sloping rack of heavy iron balls. As each arm passes C, it picks up a ball. On the opposite side of the wheel, each arm folds back on its hinges until, at point D, it gently deposits its ball back on the sloping rack. It is obvious that the extended arms with their heavy balls overbalance the wheel, which will continue turning in a clockwise direction until one of the arms gives up in exhaustion. Right?*

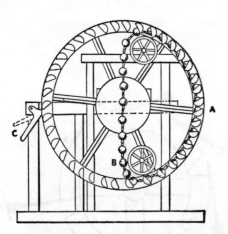

10. *You should be warned straight off that C in this drawing is a brake to keep the machine from running so fast it goes out of control. Around the outside of wheel A are cups designed to hold the iron balls (B). These balls are linked together in a chain. Since the balls take a short cut up through the center of the wheel, but the long way around the periphery on the right, there are a passel more weights on the right than on the left. The machine will turn clockwise, gradually picking up speed until it goes completely out of control unless you watch it closely and use brake C with great judgment. Why, however, won't you ever have to use the brake?*

He believed in it instantly. Here, to his mind, was real perpetual motion. Young Sellers had done what he had only claimed to do. He tried to buy out the lad, offering him a handsome share of the profits that could be made from this, the true perpetual motion.

Later in 1813, a machine identical to Redheffer's, and possibly exhibited by him, appeared in New York, and Robert Fulton, who had launched the *Clermont* six years earlier, was induced by some of his friends to visit the exhibit. Shortly after he entered, Fulton exclaimed, "Why, this is a crank motion." His sensitive ears had detected the uneven sound, induced by unequal velocity, which is typical of the motion imparted by a crank, rather than of the rotary motion implied by the machine. Fulton declared the machine a fraud and denounced the exhibitor to his face as an impostor. When the spectators became embroiled in the argument, Fulton declared that he would expose the machine or pay for any damage he did to it. Thereupon he knocked away a few thin pieces of wood which fastened the contrivance to the wall. Inside, a loop of catgut was moving at a fairly steady pace. Speculating that the gut ran up through the wall and along the ceiling above, Fulton started exploring the second floor of the building. Finally, according to his biographer, C. D. Colden, he threw open a door at the back of the house, where he discovered the true motive power—a poor old wretch with an immense beard who appeared to have suffered long imprisonment. He was unconscious of what had happened below and was seated on a stool gnawing a slice of bread which he held in one hand while turning a crank with the other. The irate mob demolished the machine, and the promoter vanished.

The infamous Keely Motor of 1874 was another perpetual-motion fraud, as well-known in its day as the equally spurious Cardiff Giant. John Worrell Keely was a good mechanic, but an even better talker; when the smooth words flowed, nearly everyone within earshot believed. In a typical demonstration, Keely would start his machine, which seemed to run on water, either by striking a tuning fork or playing a tune on a harmonica, and it would run until he stopped it. A master of scientific double talk, Keely called his mechanism successively a "vibratory generator," a "hydro-pneumatic-pulsating-vacu-engine," and an "energy liberator."

For twenty-five years the machine ran, and the smooth words flowed. Always Keely needed "just a little more money" to perfect it. He even claimed that it could propel a large ocean liner from New York to Liverpool and back on a gallon of ordinary water. His technical terms became even more mystifying and alluring, and he talked of "molecular vibration," "sympathetic equilibrium," and "oscillation of the atom."

When the fraud was at last discovered, it turned out that water indeed played its role. The house in which the machine had been demonstrated had been remodeled and contained a high-pressure hydraulic system connected almost invisibly to the machine.

As late as March, 1899, *McClure's Magazine* carried a startling article on a machine invented by one Charles E. Tripler of New York. If the machine worked (and the writer of the article seemed to underwrite its authenticity), it would make perpetual motion not only possible but almost inevitable. The writer was Ray Stannard Baker, a man who was to become something of a figure in American history—eminent author, historian, government agent, and friend and confidant of Woodrow Wilson. At the invitation of Mr. Baker, two scientists visited Tripler's laboratory for a demonstration. Though an appointment had been made, the time proved "not to be convenient" for Tripler, and the scientists never examined the machinery. There never was, indeed there never is, a convenient examination for such devices. This is almost another law of physics.

Again in 1902 a civil engineer presented a paper that implied the possibility of perpetual motion at a meeting of the American Association for the Advancement of Science.

The second law of thermodynamics is fallacious [argued the inventor]. The *effect* of an operation *can always be reversed*, and when produced by an operation which is made irreversible by the unrestrained or unbalanced action of some particular element or elements, can be reversed by another irreversible operation made irreversible by the unrestrained action of another element or elements having an opposing action to the first mentioned element or elements.

I wish to contribute the above statement to Physical Science.

It is quite a contribution.

But one kind of "perpetual motion" is, after all, quite possible. Let inventors take heart; or better, read a book by a mathematician named Mudie, published as far back as 1836, and called *Popular Mathematics*:

It is not difficult to calculate (upon mathematical principles) that if we could give any piece of matter a motion round the earth at the rate of about five miles a second, or 1,800 miles an hour, and keep up the motion at this rate, we should overcome the gravitation of that piece of matter. This is what may be regarded as the possible case of perpetual motion.

The multiplication is a little off, but who, conscious of sputniks circling the earth endlessly, can deny that this was right?

Mr. Hicks is the editor of Popular Mechanics Magazine *and a free-lance contributor to other publications.*

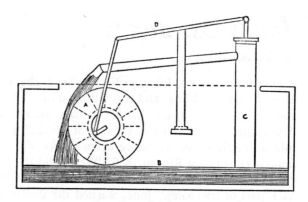

11. Here is the oldest reinvention of all. B is an enclosed basin with the water level as indicated. A is a typical water wheel, which, as it turns, operates the lever (D), drawing water up the pump (C). The water obediently goes up one side and down the other until the rig finally wears out. Yes?

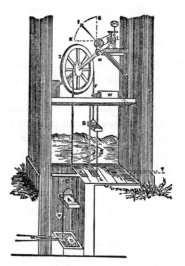

12. This machine actually was built—a magnificent structure. Beneath point X (and not shown) is a stream. A represents a large but light bucket supported by a rope over wheel Y. B represents a smaller, heavier bucket supported by a rope over wheel Z. The purpose of the machine is to raise water to reservoir W. To start it, we raise bucket A and lower bucket B to points X and E, where the stream fills them both with water. Bucket A holds more water, becomes the heavier, and descends to point D, causing bucket B to raise water to the reservoir W. A tripping mechanism then empties both buckets. Now bucket B is the heavier, so it drops back down to the stream, also raising bucket A to the stream, where both are again filled with water, and the cycle repeats itself. Other letters on the drawing merely represent refinements to impress the inventor's neighbors. Why won't this one work?

Jones vs. Jones

CONTINUED FROM PAGE 59

connection between labor radicalism and the evils of drinking, gambling, and Sabbathbreaking. "When you come down to bed-rock, all this communism and Anarchism are based upon the liquor traffic," Jones told an audience in Baltimore a few weeks after the famous Haymarket Riot in 1886. "Where did the Chicago Anarchists hold their secret conclaves? In the back part of barrooms." Jones warned the thrifty, industrious, respectable middle-class audiences which flocked to hear him, "Do you know what communism is? . . . It is the fifty thousand poor men who have been debauched by whiskey who . . . are now calling upon you to divide."

When Jones conducted a revival meeting in Chicago during the bloody riots connected with the strike at the McCormick Harvester Factory in the same year, he pointed out the implications of the parades and picnics which the workingmen of the city had organized in an attempt to raise enthusiasm and funds for their cause:

It is said Chicago has more of the Communistic element in it than any other city in America. . . . Look at your workingmen going out to some celebration. Look on the flag [they carry] and see the inscription, "Our Children Cry for Bread!" . . . A more Communistic power [slogan] was never put on a flag than that. Those same men went to the grove and drank up that day fourteen hundred kegs of beer. (Laughter) If you will put your beer-gardens and barrooms out of this city and put these millions into bread and meat you will have the fattest and plumpest children and the most prosperous city on the face of the earth. (Applause) But an old devil walking around and toting a flag saying his children cry for bread—why if you were to stick a knife in his belly four gallons of beer would run out. (Great laughter).

It was perhaps Jones's greatest contribution to revivalism that he did not, like former evangelists, look upon his crusades simply as a means of converting individuals into paragons of personal virtue and nothing more. Rather he attempted to arouse worried middle-class citizens into an army of fighting saints dedicated to stamping out the great social ills of their times. Moreover, Jones considered the mere fact of enlistment in his army tantamount to conversion. Conversion, as he defined it, was not so much a change in belief or the acquisition of grace through faith as a change in moral conduct, a resolution, as he put it, to "Quit your meanness" and to fight for decency in your community. "Conversion," he explained, "scripturally means simply two things. 1. I have quit the wrong. 2. I have taken hold of the right." Stop waiting for a change of heart, stop saying you do not feel you have got religion, he said. "You stir around and begin to right the wrongs you have done in this city. . . . You will have the feeling!" He spoke for many militant reformers of his day when he declared, "I like a broad, useful, aggressive Christianity—a Christianity with a musket and a cartridge belt. Satan won this country by fighting and we must win it back from him in the same way."

While Sam P. Jones devoted himself to reforming the country by revivalism, Sam M. Jones decided that he should try to reform the city of Toledo by entering politics. Having successfully launched his Golden Rule experiment in industrial management, the sucker-rod manufacturer entered the race for the mayoralty in 1897, hoping to give his new beliefs a wider application. As a wealthy businessman, Jones had always been a Republican, and even after his conversion to Christian socialism he did not desert his party. In fact, he was sufficiently hardheaded in his political outlook to work with the prevailing party machine in Ohio, controlled at that time by Senators Mark Hanna and Joseph Foraker. The machine, with some misgivings, gave him the Republican nomination, and Jones campaigned on a platform of "good government" and cheaper streetcar fares. His Democratic opponent, Parks Hone, tried to obscure Jones's demands for reform by accusing him of being a front for the prohibition movement. Among the beer-loving Germans and whiskey-drinking Irish who made up over one-quarter of Toledo's population, Jones's teetotalism was no asset. Nevertheless he managed to win the election by the narrow margin of 518 votes out of a total of 21,000.

To redeem one pledge of his "good government" platform, Jones made an attempt to get rid of gamblers, bookies, and slot machines, and to close the "wine rooms" where prostitutes made their headquarters. But he did not push these matters, and he put no pressure on the saloons which, according to the existing laws, were supposed to close at 11 P.M. on weekdays and all day on Sundays. Saloons, said Jones, were merely an "evidence of wrong social conditions," not their cause. He accepted the arguments that the saloon was "the poor man's club" and that the Sabbath, which was the only day off for most workingmen, was for recreation as well as for worship. Shortly after his inauguration Jones persuaded the city council to repeal the blue laws that forbade concerts and theatricals on Sunday and the ordinance requiring the saloons to close at 11 P.M. on weekdays. He could not do anything about the law requiring the saloons to close on Sunday, for this was a state law. So he simply ignored it. By this refusal to enforce Sabbatarianism he quickly brought down upon his administration the wrath of the city's clergymen and Protestant churchgoers. Six months after he assumed office, the Protestant ministers formed a committee to wait upon him and inquire why the Sabbathbreaking was allowed to continue. Jones replied that he believed the law unjust and that no more than twenty-five per cent of the city's citizens were in favor of it.

But there was even greater opposition to the Mayor's views on the current business morality, for Jones wanted to take control of public utilities out of the hands of monopolistic corporations and give them back to the people. He believed that the street railway and illuminating gas companies were mulcting the public, and he urged not only closer regulations of these concerns but eventual public ownership of them. He thoroughly overhauled the Toledo police force and, inevitably, raised the city's tax rate to provide better municipal services. As a result, those businessmen who did not already consider him unbalanced because of the way he ran his own company soon decided that he was either a crackpot, or worse, a communist. In either case, his attempt to apply the Golden Rule in municipal affairs seemed to them a deliberate subversion of the whole American way of life. By the time his two-year term of office had expired in the spring of 1899, the businessmen and the ministers of the city were solidly united against him. While the businessmen sought to persuade the Republican party to refuse Jones the renomination, the ministers set out to bring pressure upon the churchgoing public with the help of the Reverend Sam P. Jones of Georgia.

When it became known in December, 1898, that the Ministerial Association of Toledo had decided, without a dissenting vote, to ask Evangelist Jones to hold a revival meeting in their city during the month preceding the mayoralty election of April 3, 1899, a reporter was sent to talk to the ministers. Although they claimed that they were not specifically seeking to attack the Mayor, the ministers admitted that the evangelist was well known for his views on prohibition and civic reform and that "the administration of city affairs would be very likely to get a general overhauling at the hands of the noted preacher." An editorial in the Toledo *Bee* under the head, "Two Sam Joneses," remarked wrily, "There ought to be a hot time in the old town" during the next election campaign.

While the ministers were setting up committees and making general preparations in the weeks preceding the revival, the local Democrats and Republicans were holding their nominating conventions for city officers. The Democrats nominated for mayor a man named Dowling, who promised to campaign against the "haz-

Answers to
WHY WON'T THEY WORK?

1. Even if friction were no factor, this machine would waste energy. All the water must be lifted to the top, yet only part of it performs useful work on the way down.

2. If there is enough attraction to pull the magnet up the track, there will be enough to pull it to the magnet without a track. At point C the attraction is much greater than at the bottom of the track. The ball will simply fly up to the magnet, ignoring track, hole—and inventor.

3. As each bellows passes the top of the machine, it has a given amount of air which must somehow be passed down to the bellows just rounding the bottom pulley. Considerable pressure must be exerted to fill this bottom bellows under water. Eventually all bellows will have the same number of molecules of air at the same pressure, and the machine will stop.

4. The bellows must compress air into the bladders under water, which takes a significant amount of energy. The machine won't perform enough work to feed that much energy into the bellows.

5. Count the balls on the right side, as against those on the left.

6. Mercury will be pushed out of bellows at left, but will tend to run into any bellows below the pivot point. Thus all the mercury will end up in the bottom group of bellows, all vacuum in the top group.

7. Magnetic attraction pulls ball up the incline; gravity pulls it straight down. (The principle would be clearer if the inventor had drawn the magnet farther up the perimeter of the wheel.) Ball will move slightly, but will reach a point where the combination of the two forces will cancel each other out. There the wheel will stay.

8. Only two weights at the right are performing any significant amount of work, while trying to overbalance five at the left.

9. In order to deposit balls on left so they will roll down the sloping rack, they must be lifted farther than they drop.

10. If this one would work, you could run a loop of rope over a top pulley and a side pulley, and it would turn forever. Only the ball at point A is doing its full work, while all other balls on the right side are being partially supported. Yet the machine must raise the full weight of all balls moving up through the center.

11. Wasted water again, in addition to friction.

12. This is a bit unfair. The machine was built—and actually works! However, if you take a second look you will see that it is not a true perpetual-motion device, which must be a closed system operating on gravity, buoyancy, or magnetism. This machine is powered by the stream that feeds it. The flowing water performs useful work which is transmitted to the machine. Thus it operates on the same principle as a conventional water wheel.

THE DEVIL IN TOLEDO

So Said Sam Jones, the Great Evangelist, Yesterday.

HE INTENDS TO ROUT HIM

Two Large Audiences Gathered at the Armory.

HANDED OUT HOT ONES

To the "Tin Preachers" and Over Pious Sisters

POLITICIANS ARE HIT HARD

Declared They Would Sell Their Souls to Perdition in Order to Stay in Office—Today's Meetings.

Early yesterday morning it seemed as though even Sam Jones could not cope with the elements and induc... mo... ...n ... ... the "fai..."

TOLEDO Commercial, MARCH 6, 1899

Preacher Jones opened his revival before 3,000 on March 5, 1899—a month before the mayoralty election.

ardous experiments" in public ownership advocated by "Golden Rule" Jones. Jones fully expected the Republicans to renominate him; but to his dismay the party politicians chose a man named Charles E. Russell, who repudiated Jones's policies and promised to campaign on a platform calling for a "business administration." While Mayor Jones was still debating whether to admit defeat or try to run as a third-party candidate, Evangelist Jones arrived in town to start the revival.

The first meeting was held at the city Armory on Sunday, March 5. As mayor of Toledo, Samuel M. Jones was asked to say a few opening words to introduce Samuel P. Jones. Since it appeared that the Mayor would not be running for re-election, the tension over the revival had dropped. The Mayor spoke to the crowd in the Armory, saying that he was pleased to see that "a great many Toledoans were interested in the welfare of men's souls" and that he himself believed that "nothing else but the love of Christ at the heart of society" would save the world. "Things are awfully wrong now, but they are going to be right. He taught us to pray, 'Thy kingdom come.' Why then should it not come?" The Mayor concluded by saying it gave him "great pleasure to introduce to you Reverend Sam P. Jones . . ." But he added, somewhat enigmatically, "There are other Joneses."

Evangelist Jones spoke on the text, "I have fought the good fight." "The first thing to be done in Toledo," he said, "is to separate the crowd . . . we must make the issue square and draw the line. . . . You can't tell who is a church member without asking the preacher. . . . I'm here for a fight and I'm going to say things to start it. If you can say worse things about me than I can about you, just lam in, Bud. I despise a dull time."

But the evangelist did not say anything that day about civic corruption or the saloons. For the first week he devoted himself to amusing and scolding his audiences: "The Sweet Bye and Bye is all right, but I hit 'em in the Naughty Now and Now." "You have got so now in Toledo you have got to get drunk once in a while to be a gentleman." "The more dignified a preacher is the nearer dead he is." The closest his sermons got to the election campaign were such asides as: "Any town that can put up with 700 saloons is the nastiest place next to hell." And "God will bless no city that desecrates the Sabbath." He let it be known that he was neither a Democrat nor a Republican: "I'm a prohibitionist from snout to tail."

On March 9, Mayor Jones, having decided that he had sufficient popular support to give him a fighting chance for re-election, entered the mayoralty race as an Independent. To do this he had to present a petition signed by a large number. The city's two major papers (one Democratic and one Republican) noted gleefully that among the signers of his petition were "Joe Casper, the poolroom king," a gambler named Bright, and Chief of Police Raitz, who had once been caught taking a drink while on duty and who would have been fired had not Mayor Jones decided to give him another chance. This was too much for Evangelist Jones. On March 11, he told the noon prayer meeting for businessmen, "You have got three men running for mayor. . . . Just look at the gang that is following each . . . and I will tell you what kind of man he is. . . . You elect Sam P. Jones mayor of this city and I will shut up your saloons on the clock and close up your assignation houses . . . and I would hire a chief of police that would not go into a saloon and take a drop of whiskey any more than he would go into a duck pond and drown himself."

But this was mild compared to the blast the revivalist let loose the following day at a meeting for six thousand men at the Armory. The headlines in the Republican paper, the Toledo *Blade,* read: "Evangelist's Hot Shot; Jones Batteries Turned on Municipal Authorities; Declares If the Devil Were Mayor He Would Not Change a Thing." Those in the Democratic Toledo *Bee* proclaimed: "Sam P. Jones Rips Up Toledo's Administration; He Prefers Rule of Hate to the Rule of Love That Keeps the Saloons Open." Among the evangelist's remarks were these: "You have an apostle in this town who can do everything by love. My, my! If love would have regulated the laws of this town it would have taken wings and flown off long ago. Is it love that runs 700 saloons wide open seven days a week, 400 bawdy houses every night, and 150 gambling dens that carry your young and old men down to hell?"

He denounced foreigners who desecrated the Sabbath as well as the officials who let them: "For every decent German or reputable Irishman I have the hand [shake], but for a white-washed Dutchman or an anarchistic Irishman I fix my foot. If you don't like this country go back. . . . Let us have an American Sabbath and be decent." "You say I'm fooling with politics," he concluded, "I'm not. I'm naming no names, but I am running my engine on the track and if anything gets in the way it's going to be run over."

The next morning Evangelist Jones spoke at a special meeting of the co-operating pastors and laymen who met to put the churches formally into the election campaign. There it was moved that a committee of ministers try to obtain a pledge from each of the three candidates promising that if elected he would "enforce the law against the saloonists, gambling, and houses of ill fame." The motion was passed.

The Republican candidate, Russell, who had hitherto said nothing about saloons, now issued a ringing statement that if elected he would use all the authority of his office to enforce the law against "the impudent assertions of the brewers, saloons, gamblers, and brothels." Russell called upon "every good citizen" to "take off his coat and work for the home and fireside." The Democratic candidate, Dowling, hedged on the question. As expected, Mayor Jones told the ministerial committee, "It would not be consistent for me to sign a paper pledging myself to make Toledo anything more than what its citizens desire it to be. At the same time he said, "I do not believe that the extirpating method to which [the Reverend] Mr. Jones pins his faith is either the Christian or the scientific method. . . . I believe the only way in which the saloon will finally disappear will be through the growth of the loving spirit in mankind which will provide opportunity for people to live decently human lives. . . ."

But Evangelist Jones would have none of that. For

A few days later the evangelist spoke again—this time a "soul-stirring sermon" to 5,000 people.

the remainder of his stay in Toledo—which was extended from March 19 to March 22 at the request of the ministers—he continued to "draw the line" and "fire hot shots" at the Mayor in the name of decency, respectability, and Christianity. "When a man takes the oath of office to do the duties of that office, draws his salary, and does not do it, he is a perjured scoundrel in the sight of God and honest men. (Applause) If you have a law on your statute book you don't enforce, you have communism inaugurated. If you have a state law you can't enforce you have anarchy in your midst."

The city's two newspapers gave the evangelist's remarks front page headlines. If Mayor Jones's policies were continued for another two years, said the *Bee,*

Capital will immediately put Toledo on the list of municipalities to keep away from. . . . Capital isn't investing in towns that are run by theorists . . . The Golden Rule and the Declaration of Independence have nothing to do with it.

MAYOR JONES--"I Never Sought an Office."

The Toledo Blade, *opposing the Mayor's re-election, ran this cartoon in the middle of the hard-fought campaign.*

Our credit is at stake. . . . Think this over. It affects your pocket-book.

Meanwhile the *Blade* ran a series of cartoons on its front page depicting Jones as a tool of the saloon-keepers and declared editorially, "The socialism of Mayor Jones breeds anarchy."

Throughout the month of March the city's ministers (with a few notable exceptions) denounced Mayor Jones from their pulpits and called for a civic clean-up. The Reverend G. A. Burgess, a Congregationalist and a prime mover in bringing the evangelist to the city, quoted statistics in his Sunday morning sermon on March 19 to show that private ownership of public utilities was cheaper than public. "But the financial question is not the leading question," said Burgess; "moral legislation" was. Mayor Jones's failure to enforce the laws against the saloons was "anarchy."

Mayor Jones tried to counter such attacks by insisting that the moral question was a red herring. "It is a false issue raised to divert the public mind from the main question . . . the prize they are playing for is nothing less than one of the most gigantic schemes of franchise-grabbing ever concocted." As the Mayor saw it, the ministers were the dupes of "the corporate interests," particularly the city traction company, which had been out to defeat Jones from the start in order to prevent his taking over the street railways from which they made exorbitant profits.

Ironically, Mayor Jones's election campaign had, in its way, as much religious fervor as the revival meetings which Evangelist Jones was conducting at the Armory. The Mayor's good friend, the writer and future diplomat Brand Whitlock, said of his political rallies: "He was like an evangelist, in a way, and his meetings were in the broad sense religious. . . . His evangel was that of liberty." Like the evangelist, Mayor Jones had a lively sense of humor and liked a good fight. He was a good debater, and he loved to sing the campaign songs which he wrote himself to the tunes of old Welsh folk songs, Methodist hymns, or stirring marches. The words which he wrote for his campaign song of 1899 epitomized his philosophy in all its faith and optimism. It was set to a tune which may well have been selected in acknowledgment of the evangelist's part in the campaign; the tune was "Marching Through Georgia." The Mayor, however, entitled it, "Industrial Freedom."

Sing aloud the tiding that the race will yet be free,
Man to man the wide world o'er will surely
*   brothers be,*
Right to work, the right to live, let everyone agree,
God freely gives to the people.
Hurrah, hurrah! the truth shall make you free;
Hurrah, hurrah! for dear humanity.
Right to work let all proclaim, till men united be
In God's free gift to the people.

But the Mayor did not campaign on such a vague platform as this. His campaign promises included the following concrete planks: "Public ownership of all public utilities." "No grant of new or extension of existing franchises" by the city to private interests. "The abolition of the private system of doing city work." "A minimum wage of $1.50 per day for eight hours of common labor." "Organized labor to be employed on all public work."

Evangelist Sam P. Jones struck his culminating blow for righteousness at the final meeting of the revival on March 22. There were various reports of the exact words he used. Brand Whitlock quoted him as saying, "I am for the Golden Rule myself, up to a certain point, and then I want to take the shotgun and the club." The headlines of the Toledo *Bee* read: "Jones' Farewell. . . . Says Shotgun Is Better Than the Golden Rule in Politics." The version recorded by the *Bee*'s reporter had Jones saying,

I have nothing to do with politics, but I have to do with a theory that will land your town in ruin. . . . I see a mad dog coming over my fence and my wife and children are there. Do I say, "I believe in the Golden Rule for that dog?" The mad dog in this town is the saloon and the shameless houses. . . . I say the way to meet a mad dog is with a shotgun.

During the remaining week of the election campaign the Anti-Saloon League organized rallies endorsing Russell; the ministers continued to deliver sermons demanding law enforcement, and the two newspapers printed cartoons and editorials lampooning the Mayor's crackpot ideas. But all their efforts and all the words of the evangelist came to nothing. On election day Mayor Jones carried every ward in the city except one and was re-elected by a landslide. The vote was: Jones—16,733; Russell—4,266; Dowling—3,148. According to the Toledo *Blade*, the Mayor's "personal popularity" made the voters "overlook his visionary theories." "The socialistic theories of Mr. Jones, dangerous as they appear to the great mass of thinking men, appeal to a class of voters who have nothing to lose and everything to gain." The Mayor put it somewhat differently: "The people kept their minds on the one great question—Shall we have the Golden Rule of all the people or the rule of cash by a few people?"

There was no comment from the ministers, but their subsequent endorsement of other professional evangelists, like Billy Sunday, indicated that the outcome of the election had in no way affected their faith in revivalism to solve the "moral questions" of the day.

Undaunted by his evident repudiation in Toledo, Evangelist Jones continued to tour the country bringing his method of civic reform to other corrupt cities. Meanwhile the people of Toledo continued to vote for Mayor Jones and his "Golden Rule" until 1904, when he finally died in office.

In the years that followed, many Americans continued to believe, like the evangelist Jones, that meaningful reform must always begin with the individual and that the most urgent problem of the day was to prohibit the manufacture and sale of alcoholic beverages. In this respect the Toledo campaign clearly foreshadowed the passage of the Eighteenth Amendment. Inasmuch as Mayor Jones won, however, it also foreshadowed the political and economic reforms of Theodore Roosevelt and Woodrow Wilson. In the ensuing decades, the majority of Americans adopted the outlook of the mayor who believed that the American system itself needed reform. The eccentric mayor, rather than the church-sponsored evangelist, embodied the real temper of the new century.

Brother Against Brother CONTINUED FROM PAGE 7

and be assured that I hold nothing in my heart of bitterness towards you. J. D. P.

Baltimore, May 1, 1861

Dear Brother:

You are fast driving me to consider that term inappropriate.

I have received your letter of the 27th, and if you consider me a "fool and a boor" why so be it.

The only answer I have to make is that you are crazy. I will only say further that you entirely misinterpret and misunderstand the mission to Washington and what was asked of Mr. Lincoln. We asked nothing of what you so glibly ridicule.

If such is to be your correspondence it had better be stopped till you get your senses,

Yours,
J. D. Pratt

Baltimore, May 3, 1861

Dear Brother:

I am this morning advised that you have so far forgotten yourself, your personal honor, and your oft-repeated assurances of affection for me and my family under all circumstances, as to violate the confidences of private correspondence, and cause to be published a private letter, with no other intention than to influence and exasperate the public mind still farther

than it then was, and at the same time to invite and urge me to put my family under your protection.

May God forgive you for this act of dishonor and private treason.

I think I have already written you under what circumstances of excitement I wrote that first letter. I had just been overwhelmed by the sad fate of my friend, Mr. Davis, who was murdered by the troops from the North. I had seen those troops fire from the cars towards a crowd at a distance, not a man being within a hundred yards of the train; I knew nothing whatever of any mob at the other end of the city attacking the troops; I had no expectation of violence being attempted or any attempt to obstruct the passage of the troops; I did, however, hear days previous of individual threats but personally I had frowned upon such threats and did not believe that they were of any consequence whatever as I had confidence that they emanated from bad men who were but a small minority in this city: I had seen the day before (on the 18th) a body of the most miserable looking recruits pass through our city on foot under the protection of the police.[7]

[7] The day before the 6th Massachusetts was mobbed, a poorly trained regiment of Pennsylvania militia passed through Baltimore without difficulty. Its general appearance caused Lincoln's youthful secretary, John Hay, to make caustic remarks about the poor quality of the first Unionist detachments.

In a word, my heart was for peace and the Union until exasperated by the exhibition at the Washington depot and the killing of Mr. Davis, a quiet citizen, and it was under the influence of that infliction that I received your dispatch, kindly meant by you, to come away from danger and thus show myself to be a coward.

Your dispatch, kindly meant as it was, only served to increase my excitement, and I wrote you in that heated manner.

There was also another cause for my excited letter. During the intense excitement of the 19th and 20th many Northern men had been alarmed by anonymous letters from some of the mob, and I with others was named as suspicious characters.

Now, cannot you see that there was enough to madden almost any man, and cause a bitter letter to be written, which prudence and brotherly affection should have covered up and protected.

What could I think of myself if I had caused to be published your letters to me breathing forth the most fiendish threats worthy of the "dark ages." But no, I did just the contrary. I had the use of the columns of our paper here but I would suffer death before I would violate the confidence of a brother's correspondence.

When the heat of excitement had passed, and I had become acquainted with the real facts of the outbreak and violence, I admit that I was wrong and had acted and written in an improper and unchristian manner. It was some days before the people understood that the outbreak was that of a mob. Their sympathies and interests are with the South, yet they prefer the whole Union if it can be preserved peacefully.

We deplore the present thirst for blood and would if possible arbitrate for peace. This, however, is impossible so long as men and Christian men of the North breathe forth the spirit of fiendish cruelty.

All, or nearly all, in this city admit that the violence of the 19th ult. was wrong, and some days ago I suggested a paper which is now being signed, representing that in our opinion troops or whatever else the Government desire *ought* to pass through Baltimore without hindrance.

The frenzy was soon over in this city and quiet restored, and yet Christian men and women in Boston, and from your letters I suppose you with rest, instead of praying for peace, pray for blood, flames, murder, and the violation of women and children.

(Great God, what hast thou in store for this wretched country that thou shouldst permit thy professed friends to so dishonor thy cause and word!)

Did you stop to think over what the effect of this temper among Christians would be in other lands?

No, I fear not. Will they see the same spirit manifested by the South as in the North? They do not and will not. They have plead for peace: they (the border states and Virginia particularly) have exhausted all resources in their efforts to bring about a peaceable adjustment and save the *whole Union*, but they have been met by the most cruel and inhuman thirst for vengeance and blood from the North, until they were driven to desperation themselves.

For myself, I have my interests here and with the South, and also property in Virginia. I wish peace. I desire the Union, but Union in harmony, and no other is to be desired.

Oceans of blood could not harmonize or settle this question.

Now, my Brother, I close. If I have offended you it was not in my heart to do so, and I ask your forgiveness, and hard as it is to forgive your cruel offence to me and my family by the publishing and violation of private correspondence in the publishing of my letters, that particular vengeance might be brought down upon my head, I will say that I forgive you and will pray for you, but I fear you have broken the chain which should unite brothers forever and that we must part. This is a bitter cup. It cuts me to the quick and I can hardly see through my tears which flow as I write these lines.

May God forgive you.

Your brother
J. D. P.

Boston, May 6, 1861

My dear Brother:

I have just received yours of the 3rd and hasten to reply to it.

Your letter exhibits so much feeling that I begin to feel as if I had done some terrible thing. Why, Jabez, as "Old Abe" said "there is nobody hurt"; don't make yourself unhappy.[8]

The publication of the extract of your letter was wholly without thought or premeditation. I had no design to injure you and I had no thought till this moment that I had done so.

The facts are these: At the time that I received that letter there had been no mail or telegraphic communication for several days from Baltimore, and there was the utmost anxiety felt to hear from Baltimore. On the way from the office with your letter in my hand I

[8] In February, 1861, traveling from Illinois to Washington, Lincoln made a series of speeches in which he tried to allay excitement. In one of these he remarked that although several states had announced their secession, nobody had actually been hurt—a remark which both friend and foe often quoted in the weeks ahead.

Massachusetts volunteers board a train at Jersey City, bound for Washington. "Among the ladies could be seen several in tears," the New York Herald noted, ". . . and one old gentleman cried like a child."

stopped at the Journal to buy an "extra"; one of the reporters (a friend) met me and asked, "Have you heard from your brother?" "Yes" I replied, "I have this moment received a letter." "What does he say?" he asked. I replied, "Read it for yourself." He did so and then remarked that he should like to print an extract from it. After a moment's hesitation I assented, the names to be suppressed; and I had not the most remote or distant idea of doing you an injury. On the contrary, I thought you would feel complimented in being considered an exponent of public sentiment in Baltimore.

The letter has done you no harm and if you should come here today the worst that would happen would be a few harmless jokes cracked at your expense. I have heard no hard things said about you; the few who know the author think you are "plucky" and our troops would prefer to meet a *regiment* of Southerners than a *company* of Yankees; all the genuine pluck there is at the South has been transplanted from the North.

I hope, Jabez, you will consider this explanation as satisfactory. I am sorry, very sorry, if I hurt your feelings; if I did it was an error of judgment and not of the heart, and as to your publishing my letters, you are welcome to print every line I have written you in every paper in Baltimore.

I send you the extract from your letter as printed. I might send you mine if I had it at hand. However, I only printed that part having reference to the war; all that of a personal nature was left out.

As to the war, you know my sentiments. Seward's instructions to the French minister is the doctrine of the North and West. The rebellion is *to be put down, crushed out,* and *it will be done;* there is to be *one Republic* and *one only* and the dictates of true humanity are that the war should be prosecuted with all the vigor and energy possible.

As to the Christianlike spirit of the South—I have no wish to discuss that. The flames of Fort Sumter as they scorched the seventy heroes within its walls instead of appealing to human beings to stay the slaughter, appealed to fiends who revelled in the carnage and the shot of the artillery poured in as the flames rose higher. Read Major Anderson's account of the *mercy* of Southern soldiers. Is privateering a Christianlike occupation? If it is there will be a few good Christians less if our steamers catch them.

Hundreds of letters like yours have been printed in Baltimore, and the reporters of several of the papers have been after me to get letters from you to print, which I have declined. I did think of giving them that which contained the account of your interview with the President but did not do so.

You say a great many harsh things in your letter which I will not reply to, for I have no doubt you were under as great a state of excitement when you wrote this letter as when you wrote your first, and you will regret what you say in the last as you have in the first case—"dishonor," "private treachery," "heart of confidence"—hard words, but they don't apply in the present case. Your letter had reference to what was public in Baltimore. You gave me the *public* sentiment. There was nothing *private* about it and you are needlessly excited in this matter. As to bringing down upon your head "particular vengeance" in heaven's name tell me *who* has any vengeance in store for you? Where? How? I don't understand you. There is no vengeance in Boston for you, I can assure you of that, but as I said before there may be a little *fun* at your expense in the way of a *joke.* It can't be in *Baltimore,* for great as the reaction there I don't suppose the time has come when sentiments such as were contained in your first letter would hurt anybody for uttering them. Where is the "particular vengeance" coming from? It shant come. It won't come, anyhow. I will put on my Ancient and Honorable uniform [9] and with my musket and sword will defend you against all vengeance, both "particular" and general, here, in Baltimore or anywhere else. The blood of the Pratts is up and woe be to whoever stands in the way.

Now, Jabez, there is no use in getting mad or in keeping mad. Act like a sensible man and don't make such a great fuss over such a small matter. I expect you and I will make our names immortal before this contest ends, and it won't do to stop at such trifles as this.

Give my love to Lucy and all, and "through evil and good report," believe me, I am

Affectionately
J. C. P.

Boston, 6th May, 1861

My dear Brother:

I have just mailed your letter and forgot to enclose the slip from the newspaper therein referred to. I guess you won't feel bad when you see it in print.

As I told you in my letter, you may print every line of every letter I have written on this subject in every paper in Baltimore and put my name to them, and I will meet all the "particular vengeance" it brings with it in Baltimore or anywhere else.

I ought to have said in my letter in reply to your remark that we of the North were "praying for blood,

[9] The Ancient and Honorable Artillery Company of Boston was a dress-parade, high-society militia outfit that was prominent in Boston before the war.

flames, murder, and the violation of women and children" that no such prayers are offered this side of "Mason and Dixon" line. Our first prayer is that the misguided people of the South may see their folly and come back to their allegiance to the best government that the sun ever shone upon, a government without whose protection they cannot exist. Our next prayer is that the leaders in this rebellion, your Yanceys, Floyds, Davis, etc., may be arrested and hung. The next is that God would give success to our armies in crushing out the most infamous rebellion that the world ever saw.

Your women and children are safe from all except the vile creatures that horde in the South.

Yours affectionately
John C. Pratt

So the story ends. Like so many human stories, it ends in uncertainty. We do not really know whether the two brothers were fully reconciled after the war ended —whether the heated words they exchanged during the early months of the war were later buried in brotherly affection and deeper understanding. The record closes with the letters printed above.

Jabez Pratt, the Baltimore brother, appears to have died in March of 1866. His Boston brother, John C. Pratt, lived until 1888. With both brothers, the hot fires of controversy apparently died before death made the final separation. But whether the two men adjusted their differences and struck hands once more as brothers and fellow citizens . . . this, like so many other questions arising out of the Civil War, goes off into mystery.

WHAT CAUSED THE REVOLUTION?

A Few Unkind Words for Lawyers, From a Not-Unprejudiced Source

The leadership of the American Revolution was drawn from many sources—the clergy, the merchants, the planters, and the newspaper editors—but no single group was better able to articulate the colonial position within the political, legal, and constitutional framework of the Anglo-American debate than the men of the legal profession. Curiously, modern historians have done them less credit than did their contemporaries. . . .

Friends of the Crown at least were in no doubt of the legal profession's pernicious influence. "The Lawyers are the Source from whence the Clamors have flowed in every Province," General Gage assured the home government during the Stamp Act disorders. American Tories echoed the charge in their assertion that the lawyers were "cultivating, with unwearied Pains, the Seeds of Infatuation and Tumult." . . . Cadwallader Colden, New York's longtime royal lieutenant governor, . . . diagnosing the source of New York's violent disorders in connection with the Stamp Act, . . . pictured himself as the helpless victim of the lawyers' near-diabolical power:

"The Gentlemen of the Law, both the Judges and principal Practitioners at the Bar, are either Owners Heirs or strongly connected in family Interest with the Proprietors. . . . the power of the Lawyers is such that every Man is affraid of offending them and is deterr'd from makeing any public opposition to their power and the daily increase of it. . . . many Court their Friendship . . . they rule the House of Assembly in all Matters of Importance. . . .

"By this association, united in interest and family Connections with the proprietors of the great Tracts of Land, a Domination of Lawyers was formed in this Province. . . . A Domination founded on the same Principles and carried on by the same wicked artifices that the Domination of Priests formerly was. . . . Every Man's character who dares to discover his Sentiments in opposition to theirs is loaded with infamy by every falsehood which malice can invent, and thereby exposed to the brutal Rage of the Mob. Nothing is too wicked for them to attempt which serves their purposes—the Press is to them what the Pulpit was in times of Popery. . . ."

Other observers . . . conceded the accuracy of his judgment. General Gage ascribed New York City's Stamp Act troubles to the pervasive influence of the lawyers. "In this Province Nothing Publick is transacted without them." Without the instigation of the lawyers and their merchant-allies, "the inferior People would have been quiet." A young British engineering officer, stationed in the city during the disturbances, corroborated the impression. While many people of property participated in the "disloyal Insur[r]ection," he noted in his diary, the lawyers were "at the bottom" of it. They were the "Hornets and Firebrands. . . . The Planners and Incendiaries of the present Rupture."

From "Prelude to Revolution in New York: Jury Trials and Judicial Tenure," an article by Milton M. Klein in The William and Mary Quarterly, *October, 1960.*

The Red Ghost

CONTINUED FROM PAGE 37

In the course of the long voyage, however, Wayne learned so much about camels and became so thoroughly convinced that they were potentially of great value to the Army that he refused to allow such mistakes to discourage him. After landing at Indianola on May 14, 1856, he sent Porter back to the Near East for another load and drove his charges overland to the Army's Camp Verde, sixty miles northwest of San Antonio. Along the way he encountered an unanticipated difficulty—nearly every horse and mule they met bolted in terror at the sight of the beasts in his care. Since the horsemen and teamsters were enraged by this and placed all blame on the camels, it was clear to Wayne by the time he reached Camp Verde that his first task was to make converts to his point of view about the animals.

He set up a neat demonstration to that end. Assembling several of the already-hostile muleteers assigned to the experiment, he led out one of his best camels, commanded it to kneel, and loaded it with two big bales of hay, either of which would have been about as much as a mule could carry. Wayne then stepped back and surveyed the load as if afraid he might have gone too far. The onlookers muttered derisively that no animal could lift such a weight. Wayne let them convince themselves that he had made a mistake, then proceeded to add two more bales to the load. The muleteers were incredulous, and when the camel got up and strolled off at Wayne's command, they cheered. It was the sole recorded occasion on which a mule skinner expressed approval of a camel.

Wayne's only real convert was Lieutenant Edward F. Beale, one of the West's most colorful heroes. Beale's original commission was, oddly for a man identified chiefly with the western deserts, in the U.S. Navy, in which he had enlisted in 1836 at the age of fourteen. In 1846 he and Kit Carson had rescued the U.S. troops besieged near San Diego by crawling through the Mexican lines to bring help. Another of his famous exploits had been carrying the first gold from Sutter's Mill in California overland to Washington, D.C.

During and after the Civil War he was to serve as a Union general and as minister to Austro-Hungary. He was the sort of man to whom new ideas appealed, and having resigned his Navy commission in 1851 to devote himself to western exploration, he accepted, at Wayne's urging, an Army lieutenancy and appointment to the Camel Corps.

After several months of training with the camels, Beale was assigned to survey a route from Fort Defiance, New Mexico, to the eastern frontier of California, across the deserts of New Mexico and Arizona. For the expedition he chose twenty-five of the best camels from Wayne's herd and from the additional forty-four brought in on the second trip by Porter. By the time he had completed the survey of what is now approximately the route of the western half of the famous highway, U.S. 66, he was convinced that the camel was the solution of the Southwest's transportation problem.

"My admiration for the camels increases daily with my experience of them," he wrote in the official report of the survey which he submitted in the spring of 1858. True, in his report Beale allowed his affection for the animal to influence him. He had become so fond of camels that he even learned a bit of Arabic on the theory that they might be homesick for that language. One big white camel, which stood eight feet high at the hump and which he called Seid, was his favorite mount, and he gave it more care than most frontiersmen gave their horses. But there was also undoubted justice in his claims for the camels. By careful experiment he had established that in nearly any kind of terrain to be found in the Southwest, three camels could carry on their backs as much as six mules could pull in a wagon and cover the ground nearly twice as fast. Furthermore, when the expedition forded the Colorado River from Arizona into California, all the camels swam it with ease, but a dozen horses and mules were swept away by the current and drowned. And, as a final test, at the end of the journey Beale took a dozen camels north from Los Angeles into the Sierra Nevada, and found them readily adaptable both to high altitudes and to cold weather.

All this finally convinced the War Department. In December, 1858, John B. Floyd, who had succeeded Jefferson Davis as Secretary of War, formally declared the experiment a success and recommended to Congress the importation of a thousand more camels. By then, however, Congress was too busy with the preliminaries to the Civil War to give the matter any consideration. This was fortunate for the animals that might have been brought over, since the camels already on hand were finding themselves strangers among men for whom strangeness justified utter barbarity.

Major Wayne and Lieutenants Beale and Porter seem to have been very nearly the only Americans who understood and valued the animals, and when war neared, all three were transferred to duty in the eastern part of the country. They left behind only three others who had any appreciation of the camels' potential usefulness. These were three remarkable Levantines who had been signed on by Lieutenant Porter during his second and final camel-buying trip to the Near

East. All of them apparently knew at least a little about camels when hired, were able to learn more, and eventually became the Army's most expert camel handlers. One was a Turk named Elías, who ultimately settled across the border in Sonora and whose son, Plutarco Elías Calles, was to become Mexico's president and strong man in the 1920's. The other two, Georges Xaralampo, a Greek, and Hadji Ali, a cheerful Arab who came to be known affectionately as Hi Jolly, stayed with the Army for many years and tried repeatedly to convince others of the camel's value. They had little success, but Hi Jolly became so widely known and so closely identified with his charges that Arizona officials eventually erected a commemorative monument over his grave and topped it with an effigy of a camel.

This was many years after the little Arab's death, when the camels had become only a vague, colorful memory. Such a monument would have been inconceivable to the men whom Wayne, Beale, and their Levantine helpers tried to train as camel drivers. To nearly every cowhand and mule skinner who came in contact with them, the camels were incomprehensible abominations, and the feeling was mutual. Camels are among the most thoroughly domesticated animals, but they take knowing. To their North African and Asiatic owners they are of such value that they are treated with care and respect. Unlike the horses, mules, and cattle to whom the southwestern cowhands were accustomed, they have highly effective means of retaliating when they do not receive such treatment.

The legend of the old-time cowboy's affection for his horse is in large part a Hollywood invention. Owen Wister included in the first draft of one of his stories an incident in which an enraged cowhand gouged out the eyes of a horse. He was begged by Theodore Roosevelt to delete the scene, not because it was unrealistic but because it might "encourage cruelty to animals." Even sane riders often brutalized their mounts unmercifully. And mule skinners were so called with good reason; they were quite capable of removing bits of the animals' hides with the weighted whips they used. But when anyone tried to treat camels in this way, he got back as good as he gave. There were many repetitions of a little set-to which took place at Camp Verde in Texas soon after the first camels arrived.

One of the Army muleteers was practicing loading a camel and piled on too much to suit the beast. It groaned and complained in the usual camel fashion and refused to rise. The muleteer kicked it in the belly. The camel turned its head and spat full in his face a huge and foul-smelling wad of cud. Wild with rage, the muleteer grabbed a club and swung at the

The two-humped Bactrian camel originated in ancient Persia.

animal's head. The camel dodged easily, emitted a shrill, hair-raising scream, and raked the man's arm to the bone with its great, tusklike incisors.

That encounter was the beginning of an unremitting war on the camels by the Army's mule skinners. Nothing could have been better designed to enrage such men than the camels' habit of spitting copiously and accurately on anyone rousing their resentment. This means of reprisal, together with the animals' ways of moaning and groaning at being loaded and their seemingly haughty, disdainful expression, made many of those employed to handle them hate them to the point of obsession.

Besides hating the camels for their looks and lack of proper docility under harsh treatment, the cavalrymen despised them as foreign. This is ironic, because camels were American for millions of years before any member of the human family showed up in this hemisphere. The whole camel family, like the horse family, evolved here and spread to the eastern hemisphere via the then well-traveled land bridge from Alaska to Siberia a mere million years ago. One species of true camel persisted in California until fifteen thousand years ago, and the South American branch, which includes the llamas and vicuñas, still flourishes. Some of the latter are the only members of the family still persisting in the wild state, all the Old World camels having long since submitted to the domestication process that began before the dawn of history.

By the time of his transfer to the East, Lieutenant Beale had come to realize that the men's attitude toward the camels was the chief obstacle to his plans. Because he had become fond of the animals and had learned how to handle them, he knew that they could be, as he phrased it, "so quiet and docile that frequently we forget they are with us." But he found it impossible to leave them with the men without his personal supervision. Even harsh punishment of teamsters caught mistreating the camels had little effect.

"The Americans of the class who seek such employment," Beale wrote in a letter to Floyd, "are totally unfit for it, being for the most part harsh, cruel and impatient with the animals entrusted to their care." He advised hiring Mexicans to manage the beasts.

But Beale soon was transferred, and his suggestion was ignored. His departure actually ended the experiment, although the Army took a while to make abandonment of it official. When he left, the camels were scattered among military posts from Texas to California, and the men unwillingly in charge of them had little trouble arranging for their "escape" a few at a time into the desert. When the project was formally abandoned in 1863, those left to be auctioned off in California numbered only thirty-odd.

Meantime, several San Francisco mining magnates had organized a company for the purpose of importing camels for use in Nevada. These men had heard something of the Army's troubles with its camels and thought they had an explanation for it—namely, that the one-humped dromedary of the Near East that the Army had picked was the wrong kind of camel. The proper camel for the American West, they thought, was the two-humped Bactrian from the Mongolian deserts of the Far East. The records do not name the man who sold the mine owners this bill of goods. San Francisco abounded in confidence games in those days, and this was a minor operation. Its result was the importation from China of twenty Bactrians which were driven across the mountains to be put to work hauling salt from the southern Nevada marshes to the Virginia City refineries.

Harper's New Monthly Magazine, OCTOBER, 1857

The one-humped dromedary, a native of Arabia.

The profit motive quickly proved as ineffective as army discipline in restraining the reaction to the camels of the men hired to handle them. Although the Bactrians were a little stronger and heavier than Beale's dromedaries and thus capable of bearing still bigger burdens, they were no less resentful of mistreatment. Once a teamster became enraged at one of the animals when it succeeded in ridding itself of most of what it considered an overload. The man grabbed the beast's halter and attempted to beat it into submission as he would have beaten a mule. Instead of submitting, the camel went berserk and trampled him to death before his friends could shoot it.

This camel was the most fortunate of the imported Bactrians. Many of the others had to endure months of mistreatment before succumbing. Some of the mistreatment, however, was the result more of ignorance than of malice. To the camel handlers the legend that the animals store great quantities of water in their humps was a matter of unquestioned fact, and it meant that so long as the humps seemed intact the camels needed no watering. In all likelihood many of the Bactrians died of thirst.

The legend about water storage in the hump was imported with the camels from their Asian homes. Apparently Beale accepted it, too, but he and the Asian camel owners did not permit that belief to overrule their common sense. Their camels were of great value to them, and they knew from experience that even when the humps were big and firm the animals sometimes still needed water. Beale learned this through observation. His camels could go much longer than mules without water and on occasion would refuse it when offered, but at other times, even though their humps were in fine shape, they drank deeply.

The hump legend, or the alternative one that a camel stores water in one of its three stomachs, still is widely accepted. The latter is cited as fact in at least one recent and generally authoritative work on natural history. Only in the last decade have two young researchers in comparative physiology, Drs. Knut and Bodil Schmidt-Nielsen, a husband-and-wife team, finally uncovered the truth. The camel's hump is fat and contains no extra moisture, and the supposed water in the little sacs lining one of its stomachs is digestive fluid. The true reasons for the camel's ability to go without drinking for an unusual period under certain conditions are two: its body temperature can vary widely, and it can tolerate great dehydration.

In hot weather and under exertion, most mammals must lose moisture via perspiration in order to keep their body temperatures within a certain range. Evaporation of sweat has a cooling effect. A human being, for instance, functions properly only when his body stays within about one degree of 98.6 degrees Fahrenheit. When outside temperature pushes it toward the upper limit, he perspires faster and loses more moisture to counteract the rise. A camel, on the other hand, instead of sweating to prevent a rise in its body's temperature simply absorbs heat during the day and radiates it at night. Its temperature varies from 93 degrees in the predawn coolness to 104 degrees in midafternoon.

♞ It still may have to sweat to some degree, though at a far slower rate than most other animals, in order to stay within the upper limit. If it carries heavy burdens during the heat of the day, it may lose sizable amounts of moisture. A man can stand losing water amounting to only about ten per cent of his body weight. A camel can lose water amounting to more than thirty per cent of its body weight without much accompanying loss of strength.

It is because it is adapted in these ways to desert life that the camel is able to carry heavy loads for as long as four days without water, as Beale accurately observed. Given lush, moist pasturage and comparatively cool weather, the animal has been known to go as long as four months without a drink, being able to obtain all the necessary water from the grass. But under the conditions in which they worked in Nevada, four days probably was near the limit. Pushed beyond that, some of the Bactrians fought wildly for their lives and were shot; others plodded stoically on until they collapsed and died.

With the death of the Bactrians, the dromedaries auctioned off by the Quartermaster at Benicia Arsenal in California and a few others that previously had strayed or been driven from army posts were the only remnants of the experiment still in Union territory. (Another group of the animals somehow survived the war behind Confederate lines in Texas but was quickly scattered afterwards among circuses and zoos.) The man who bought those auctioned at Benicia, Samuel McLeneghan, hired the little Arab, Hi Jolly, to help drive the animals to Nevada and tried to put them to the salt-hauling the Bactrians had been doing, but the freighters who had regained the contract for the work wanted no more camel competition. At their behest the state legislature outlawed the use of camels on public roads on the grounds that they frightened horses and mules. McLeneghan and Hi Jolly drove the animals back south to Yuma in the Arizona Territory where McLeneghan disappeared, leaving them on Hi Jolly's hands. He managed to eke out a living for a while by using the camels to haul water out along the driest stretches of the wagon road where he could sell it to thirsty travelers, but he, too, gave up some-

time in the late 1860's and turned the animals loose.

Thereafter, the more fortunate of the camels were on their own. Since they were the product of several thousand years of domestication, being left to fend for themselves in the desert was a hard fate, but it was far better than what happened to those that occasionally were recaptured. Every now and then a group of prospectors or cowhands would run across a camel. In most cases they simply used it for target practice. Sometimes an enterprising freighter would make an abortive attempt to put a few of the beasts back to work. But inevitably, some of the animals fell into the hands of sadists who found more imaginative uses for them.

This was the apparent fate of the one which came to be known as the Red Ghost. It seems the only possible explanation of the burden it bore on its back. In the early days of the Ghost's notoriety, it was generally believed that the corpse was that of a traveler who had tied himself there as he grew weak from thirst, hoping that the camel would take him to water. But when it ultimately became possible to examine the animal, it was found that the rawhide strips which had held the burden in place could not have been tied the way they were by the man who was that burden.

"The only question," editorialized the *Mohave County Miner*, "is whether the man was tied on for revenge or merely as an ugly piece of humor by someone who had a camel and a corpse for which he had no use."

The question, that is, was whether the man was still alive when lashed to the animal's back. If he were still living, hatred of the camel presumably was not the sole motive for the exploit. It is a nice point and doubtless never will be settled. But whether the man was alive or dead, it is clear that whoever tied him on the camel was a white man. The Apaches and other Indians of the area had many practices that seem to us cruel, such as killing captured infants, but they would never have considered wasting such a supply of meat as a camel.

♞ Whoever did the deed succeeded in making the camel suffer, but like most members of its species, it refused to suffer in silent resignation. Although it killed only once, it attacked human beings nearly every time it encountered them during the first months of its agony. One of the few occasions on which it fled instead of attacking was when it was fired on by the party of prospectors who sighted it near the Verde River. A few days later a freighter halted his string of wagons for the night on the banks of the Verde some miles to the north. There were several kegs of whiskey in the cargo, a fact that may help account for some of the details of the reports the freighter and his helpers later gave concerning the events of that night.

As they told it, they had unhitched and hobbled their mules and were bedded down for the night when the comfortable silence was abruptly rent by an unearthly scream. A great beast which they estimated to be at least thirty feet high flapped down into their midst on black wings that covered nearly the whole sky. Its landing jarred the ground like an earthquake and knocked over two of the wagons. Terrified men and mules scattered in all directions, including into the river. When the men crept back to their camp the next morning, the only bits of evidence they could find were the prints of huge, cloven hoofs and a few red hairs sticking to one of the overturned wagons.

It is possible that some other depredations attributed to the camel in the following months were the work of other animals, of pranksters, or of the imaginations of the victims. To it were laid such feats as breaking into isolated cabins, caving in mine entrances, and stampeding cattle or horses. Only the last seems likely: the sight or smell of a camel always panicked horses and mules even in broad daylight until they had spent enough time around the humped creatures to get used to them.

The last known occasion of a violent encounter between the Red Ghost and a man occurred nearly a year after the camel had trampled to death the woman at Eagle Creek. One evening just at dusk a cowhand employed on the Anchor-JOT ranch east of Phoenix happened to ride past a branding corral used only at roundup time. That time was a long way off, and the corral should have been empty. It wasn't. The cowhand rode up to the corral's open gate to investigate the odd animal browsing inside.

It happened that the man had his lariat out. When the animal in the corral caught sight of him and came charging out, he automatically lassoed it. Not until he had the rope around its neck did he realize that his quarry was a camel. There was no time then for regrets.

His horse either was extremely well-trained or simply had no chance to bolt. Instead, it reared on its hind legs and pirouetted as it had been taught to do in avoiding a roped steer. But the camel did not pass harmlessly by as any bovine would have done. It crashed head on into the off-balance horse, and mount and rider went down together. With scarcely a break in stride the camel passed over them and on into the night. But even in the moment of terror the cowhand noticed that the camel still bore on its back the remnant of a burden which once had been a man.

That was not only the camel's last attack but also the last report of anyone's noticing the grisly pack it bore. In all likelihood it was able to rid itself of the remainder soon after this. With it the Red Ghost lost the goad that had driven it to violence and the unmis-

takable evidence that distinguished it from others of its species. As the years passed, it faded slowly from terrifying reality into a story to frighten tenderfeet with.

If that had been the end of the matter, it probably would have been forgotten long since or classed as just another of the West's tall tales. But almost ten years after first being noticed, the Red Ghost made a final appearance. The *Mohave County Miner* reported the incident on February 25, 1893.

THE PHANTOM THAT TERRIFIED ALL ARIZONA FOR A TIME

Another ghost is laid. Another of the tribe of gaunt hobgoblins that keep the romance of the mysterious southern deserts is gone. Another of the unearthly dangers that the timid Mexican women used to pray against has departed.

Mizoo Hastings of Ore was the priest that exorcised this phantom. Mizoo has a ranch a little above the gold camp on the San Francisco River. He woke up one morning and saw through the window of his cabin a big red camel banqueting in his turnip patch. Mizoo took a dead rest on the window sill and blazed away. He got the camel.

When he went out to examine the beast, he found that he was all scarred up and had evidently had a very hard time. He was covered with a perfect network of knotted rawhide strips. They had been on him so long that some of the strands had cut their way into the flesh.

That also was very nearly the end of the story of the camel in the American desert—but not quite. One historian of the Southwest will assure you that the last authentic sighting of a camel was reported by a crew surveying the international boundary between Arizona and Mexico in 1901. Another is convinced that an Atchison, Topeka & Santa Fe crew told the truth about seeing one near Wickenburg, Arizona, in 1913. A third is intrigued by reports of a camel's stampeding horses near Banning, California, twenty-five miles west of Palm Springs, in 1929. In 1941 there was a report from the territory east of the Salton Sea. In 1957 I met a part-time prospector, part-time guide, and all-round desert rat who, although he himself had never seen one, was sure that camels still ranged deep in the burnt hills of Sonora and Baja California. These rumors are like ghosts of the Red Ghost, faint but lingering reminders of the kind of horror members of our species alone can perpetrate and of the remarkable powers of endurance of other forms of life.

Robert Froman, who has written widely for many magazines, is also the author of One Million Islands for Sale. *"The Red Ghost" is taken from his new book,* The Nerve of Some Animals, *published this month by Lippincott.*

READING, WRITING, AND HISTORY

By BRUCE CATTON

The Sense of Wonder

Something valuable went out of the world when the last blank spaces on the map were filled in. The age-old area of myth and fable, which had helped to condition men's minds ever since men first had minds to develop, shrank to the vanishing point, and an odd constriction of the human spirit seems to have begun. Western man lost his sense of wonder; his world became smaller than it had been, and having no more room for surprises it appeared also to have less room for opportunity.

Perhaps all that had happened was that Western man grew up. Knowing more about the world, he began to realize—as any youth does, when he gets on into full manhood—that most of the infinite possibilities which once beguiled him were simply part of a mirage. Yet growing up is a painful process, even a crippling one. The ultimate horizon turns out to be nearer than had been supposed, and what lies beyond it will be about what lies on this side. The universe hereafter is just a little less stimulating.

The loss of that sense of wonder may have odd effects. As far as Western man is concerned it seems to have been accompanied by a certain loss of drive, almost a loss of vitality. One of the great characteristics of the age of exploration and discovery which dawned in western Europe five centuries ago was the unbounded energy that it evoked. The lid was off, and anything could happen. Western man had a sense of destiny; facing the unknown, he had a bubbling confidence that he could master anything he might dis-

cover. Precisely because the world was so uncertain, he developed an enormous certainty about the part he himself was going to play.

So small nations attempted great things. There was Portugal, for instance: a minor nation, menaced by Spain and by the Moslems, poor, with a scanty population scratching a living from an inadequate countryside and with no visible prospects worth betting on. Yet it was Portugal that led the way in the great break-through, opening the sea road to the East, de-

---

Prelude to Empire: Portugal Overseas Before Henry the Navigator, by Bailey W. Diffie. University of Nebraska Press. 127 pp. $1.95.

---

veloping the ships and the men with which the unknown was first approached, producing such world figures as Henry the Navigator and Vasco da Gama, and incidentally winning for itself a fabulous empire half a world away. The slow development, in this unpromising land, of the knowledge, the skill, and above all the energy which made all of this possible is succinctly detailed by Bailey W. Diffie in a meaty little book called *Prelude to Empire*, which sheds an interesting light on the way in which the business got started.

Portugal, to repeat, started with nothing much except a very old seafaring tradition and a strategic location on one of the world's early trade routes. Before the Renaissance, ships from the Mediterranean were going out past Gibraltar to carry goods to France and the Low Countries, clinging to the coast as they went,

FROM *The Journal of Christopher Columbus*

In frail caravels like this one and those on the opposite page, sixteenth-century sailors faced the ocean's terrors.

calling at the sea towns of Portugal. Portuguese exporters contributed their own goods, and Portuguese ships carried their share, and the nation began to see that its future lay on the open sea. But there were problems. Sea-borne commerce then was an odd mixture of piracy, hot-and-cold war, and commercial chicanery. The ocean was cold, rough, and cruel; to trade by sea and survive at all called for a genuinely unusual combination of talents.

The Portuguese made it. Most of the time, as the author of this book makes clear, they were thinking about nothing much more than the business of making a living. Yet their picture of the world began to expand. You trade with the Low Countries, with England, with Genoa, with North Africa, and bit by bit you get a new idea. The sea is a highway rather than a barrier; with all of its desperate hazards it is a way into a broader universe; get tough, figure all of the angles, develop better ships, sharper merchants, more daring princes—and in the end you may have a great deal more than you thought about when you started.

So the far horizon became a challenge rather than a limitation. Trying to do no more than make a profit, the traders and adventurers of Portugal (the two had to be one and the same, just then) found themselves bringing on the great age of discovery. They developed the caravel, the ship that could go far with few hands at low expense, a fit instrument for men who wanted to go beyond the curving edge of the known world; they developed also the body of knowledge that would be needed for the great explorers; and with all of this they generated an immense driving force that would not be satisfied with the trade to the Low Countries but that would insist on surpassing the bounds of the known and familiar. As Mr. Diffie remarks: "There was energy to spare in Portugal. The question was not *if* it would burst out, but when and where."

This uprush of energy, of vital force, of daring and know-how and hard determination, grew out of the simple business of trying to make a living at sea. Sea captains wandered to places we still do not know about, came back and deposited the odds and ends of their knowledge with wealthy patrons or in waterfront taverns, talked vaguely of far-off islands no one else had seen, and of the possibilities that might come if a seafaring man shot the works—and suddenly this small nation was ready to lead the Western world into a new era where the possibilities, at least for a few generations, would be infinite.

The break-through came in 1415, when Portugal somehow found the resources and the driving force to seize the Moslem stronghold at Ceuta, in Africa. Ceuta was not far away, but it was a first step; beyond it, down the coast, was the western bulge of the continent, beyond that was the cape, and beyond that was the road to the East, the road to an illimitable expansion of the European horizon, the open road to everywhere. Nobody was quite ready to take this road in 1415; but this small nation was ready for the great Henry, for serious attention to what might be done beyond the known seas, for Vasco da Gama and what came after him. Thinking to do no more than survive, these people accomplished something far greater than they had intended.

Moment of Dawn

And so, of course, did Christopher Columbus. This greatest and most fascinating of all explorers went looking for a short cut to the East and found instead the infinite West; and although he never quite realized what he had done—the enormous dimensions of his achievement were in fact too big for any of his contemporaries to grasp—he was very well aware that he had sailed out of one era and into another, and that nothing again would ever be quite the same. He compelled men to remake all of their maps, a process which would last for four centuries and more, and the business changed the mapmakers as much as it changed the maps. Mankind behaves differently when the world grows larger. It finds new capacities and develops the urge to use them.

Naturally, it is impossible for anyone today to know precisely what was in Columbus' mind when he made that first voyage. Yet it is not altogether a mystery, for the man did keep a journal, and although this has not survived, we do have an abstract made by the Dominican Bartolomé de las Casas, who appears to have consulted the original and to have copied certain parts of it. Las Casas introduced some material of his own, for which he was later criticized, but by and large his manuscript is accepted as being fairly faithful to the spirit of Columbus' own work; and an excellent edition of *The Journal of Christopher Columbus*, translated by Cecil Jane, with a foreword by L. A. Vigneras and an appendix by R. A. Skelton, has recently been published.

Out of these jottings we can at least see that as he sailed from island to island on the far side of the ocean, Columbus was forever bemused by a sense of wonder. The entries in his log become lyrical; over and over he assures the King and Queen of Spain (to whom he delivered his log book, on his return to Spain) that no one who was not actually present could understand how marvelous it all was.

"There are fish here," Columbus writes, "so unlike ours that it is a marvel . . . and the colors are so fine that no man would not wonder at them or be anything but delighted to see them." And again: "I walked among the trees, and they were the loveliest sight I have yet seen . . . and all the trees are as different from ours as night is from day, and so is the fruit and the grasses and the stones and everything else. . . . Your Highnesses may believe that this is the best and most fertile and temperate and level and good land that there is in the world."

In places Las Casas summarizes what Columbus wrote instead of making a direct copy, and the same boundless enthusiasm comes through: "The admiral says that he had never seen anything so beautiful. All the neighborhood of the river was full of trees, lovely and green, and different from ours, each one with flowers and fruit after its kind." The people who lived on these islands seemed to Columbus to have come unstained from creation's dawn: "They are . . . a people very free from wickedness, and unwarlike . . . they are very gentle and do not know what it is to be wicked, or to kill others, or to steal." The conquista-

dors who followed Columbus would give these luckless folk a liberal education in some of these matters, but in the hour of discovery Columbus certainly understood that he had entered a new world, even though he believed it to be part of Japan or China.

The very word "wonder" appears over and over, even where Las Casas is departing from the text of the original. Columbus, says Las Casas at one point,

---

The Journal of Christopher Columbus, translated by Cecil Jane, with a foreword by L. A. Vigneras and an appendix by R. A. Skelton. Clarkson N. Potter, Inc. 227 pp. $7.50.

---

tells his sovereigns that "they must not wonder that he praises all so much, because he assures them that he believes he has not said the hundredth part. . . . Finally he says that if he who has seen it feels so great wonder, how much more wonderful will it be to one who hears of it, and that no one will be able to believe it if he has not seen it."

It is no mere figure of speech to say that the age of wonder developed when the great discoveries were made. The wonder brought desire, and the two together generated an incalculable energy; Western man

FROM *The Journal of Christopher Columbus*

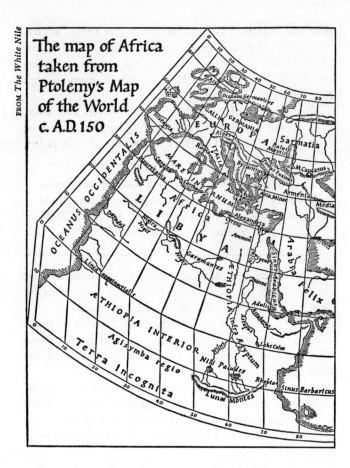

The map of Africa
taken from
Ptolemy's Map
of the World
c. A.D. 150

ern day fell upon the last recesses of the dark continent. Richard Francis Burton, Captain James Grant, and John Hanning Speke, abandoning the old effort to go up the Nile from Egypt, cut cross-lots from Zanzibar and got into the area of Africa's great lakes. They were followed, presently, by Sir Samuel Baker, and then by Dr. David Livingstone and the slightly incredible Henry M. Stanley; after which, in the fullness of time, came General Charles George Gordon, who was killed at Khartoum. The great era of privately financed expeditions came to an end, and the European governments took over; General Kitchener led

---

The White Nile, by Alan Moorehead. Harper & Brothers. 385 pp. $5.95.

---

an army up the Nile and broke native power in the Sudan, accompanied—so recent was all of this, and so long is one man's life span—by a brash young man named Winston Churchill. By the end of the century the Nile was known and was open (controlled, incidentally, all the way to Central Africa by Great Britain), and the great age of exploration had just about come to its close.

Yet somehow it is what happened afterward that is most particularly interesting. The world today looks very different from the way it looked in 1900, and nowhere is the difference more striking than in Africa. Awaiting final exploration, Africa, as far as any man could tell, was simply one more sizable portion of the earth which Western society would first examine, then control, and at last exploit; and it went without saying that the exploitation would benefit not only Western society but the Africans themselves. Africa would be given the blessings of modern civilization, its age-old evils would be reformed—contemplating the atrocious slave trade, Dr. Livingstone called down Heaven's blessing on any outsiders "who will help to heal this open sore of the world"—and in the not-distant future the whole continent would be enfolded in the dynamic and forever expanding system of the Western world.

The men who played their parts in the whole operation were almost fantastically unlike one another, but they did have one thing in common: a deep sense of mission, of destiny, of certainty. They might have had doubts about what they would find when they reached the sources of the Nile, but they had no doubts at all about either the rightness of what they were trying to do or the permanence of the new regime which, in one way or another, they were bringing to this newly opened country. The old vitality which had transplanted Western institutions to the New World and had asserted control over the Orient was still at work;

acquired a profound certainty in his own destiny, and went on to become (for a time at least) master of all the world. It began then. Where did it end?

End of the Road

It ended, apparently, in Africa, just about a century ago, and no one who had anything to do with it thought for one moment that anything was ending. On the contrary, men supposed that a new threshold had been crossed, and that more doors would be opened as the years went on. But the last blank places on the map were at last being filled, and without any warning at all the old driving energy went to seed. The moment of final triumph was also the beginning of the end. The great age of discovery was flickering out; as it did so, Western man's confidence, his inbred certainty that he and no one else was in charge of what was going to happen to the world, began to flicker out with it. It took a century for this fact to become apparent, but the process was at work.

This comes through in Alan Moorehead's excellent *The White Nile*, which covers roughly the last fifty years of the nineteenth century, when the Nile was finally traced to its source, and the broad light of mod-

what had happened in other places would assuredly happen here. Africa would be a useful and rewarding member of the European community.

As it turned out, Africa had other ideas. So, in the course of a few decades, did the European community. The Nile is indeed open, but it is not under the sort of control which the explorers envisaged. The serene confidence that this immense continent would provide new bases for empires has all but entirely evaporated; if Western man today can be said to have a settled thought in regard to Africa it can be expressed in the simple question: "What on earth is going to happen next?"

It would of course be a violent over-simplification to say that the limitless energy with which Western society went about the business of shaping the world to its own liking ran thin just because the age of exploration ended and the map was filled in to the last

As Ferdinand and Isabella bid him farewell, Columbus departs for the New World. This 1621 engraving probably depicts his second voyage, in 1493, or his third, in 1498.

remote township. A good many things happened to that energy. A great deal of it was exhausted in the terrible convulsion of the First World War, and more of it was dissipated in the confused and frantic generation that followed. Opening the dark places of the earth, Europeans and Americans gave to the people living in those places a new notion of how life there might be transformed; a new notion, and a certain aptitude for having a try at it. Without realizing that they were doing it, the Westerners released more energy than they could control; at the same time the West came to see that it had problems at home which were immediate and pressing enough to absorb all of society's vital forces for some time to come. If the broad expectations of the last of the great explorers and exploiters came to much less than was anticipated, there are solid reasons for it.

Yet no one will ever again see what the early navigators saw when they ventured without charts into seas which might contain unimaginable marvels and mysteries, what the weary explorers saw when they first looked on the sources of the Nile, on the empty plains beyond the Missouri, or on the lonely river that goes north from Great Slave Lake; and because no one will ever look at anything on earth in just that way, something behind the eye of the beholder has undergone a subtle change. Where does the sense of wonder come from, and what does it do when it possesses a man? What happens when it leaves? Does energy then die?

Cause and effect, or just happenstance?

A New Horizon?

The idea is worth dwelling with for a while. Suppose, just for the sake of supposing, that something happens to push the horizons back once more, to restore the old feeling that we live in a world of infinite possibilities. What then takes place back in the adrenal glands? Do we then, in other words, find the dynamic force that goes with the unlimited view? Do the two actually go together?

Ernest S. Dodge has written a book called *Northwest by Sea*, which examines some of the steps which were taken, or at least attempted, back at the very dawn of the great age of exploration—the efforts to find a way through or around the unknown American continents, the search for the Northwest Passage, the long struggle to determine whether America was an obstacle or an opportunity or possibly a blend of both. It has a haunting overtone.

In the beginning, of course, America was simply in the way. Following the discoveries of the Portuguese and of Christopher Columbus, the other nations began to take to the sea lanes, looking for an open road to the fabled Orient. The American continents lay across their path, but for generations Europeans were unable to believe that an open highway did not exist. They prowled up into every sound, bay, and estuary on both continents, always hopeful and always disappointed; then, at last, they tried the northern route, and from John and Sebastian Cabot down to Roald Amundsen they looked for the channel by which wind-driven ships could travel east by sailing west. What they were looking for was not there, but it took them nearly four centuries to assimilate that hard fact.

In the course of those centuries some great voyages were made; and it is mildly interesting to note that an odd sort of international brotherhood of technicians developed, men who knew the job but who were not firmly tied to any one nation. The technicians might be Spanish, Portuguese, Italian, Dutch, French, or British; they sailed, off and on, for just about anyone who wanted a voyage made; their knowledge of seamanship, of the open ocean, and of the inadequate body of knowledge that was sole guide for men who wanted to sail over the top of the world was an international resource that could be tapped by any sovereign or trading guild that had money to spend. From the day of the caravel down to the day of the atomic-powered submarine, they kept at it, adding immeasurably to mankind's store of wisdom about this planet, bringing the unattainable horizon down to the place where it could be charted, sounded, and made familiar, finding no Northwest Passage they could use . . . and at last running out of mystery and anything-can-happen into the workaday world which makes up the middle of this distressing twentieth century.

They had, in full measure, that sense of wonder, that ability to believe which survives because the solid reason for skepticism has not yet taken firm root. They discovered the authentic horn of the unicorn, which unhappily turned out to be the broken tusk of a narwhal. They found gold on the ghastly shores of Davis Strait, and only later did they learn that their ore was nothing but worthless iron pyrites. They saw attractive mermaids in the polar seas, and wrote about them with such convincing detail that we would be sure they really had seen mermaids if the years had not taught us better. In the end, they learned too that the sea lane they were hunting for was so clogged with ice and with danger that no one would ever be able to use it. They went to the end of North America and also to the end of mystery and fantasy, and when they had finished their amazing voyages, the world had shrunk to proper size, had become prosaic and familiar, and had become ever so much less stimulating. They gave us, in short, the modern world, which has

room neither for marvels nor for the belief that marvelous things can happen, a world in which the human spirit is less expansive and less vigorous than it used to be.

This they left for us, and the great age of exploration is over. And yet . . . a faint tingling in the scalp, a quiver along the back of the neck, sets in just as we reach the end of this chapter. For, as Mr. Dodge remarks, the Northwest Passage has at last become a per-

Northwest by Sea, by Ernest S. Dodge. Oxford University Press. 348 pp. $6.50.

fectly feasible passage for a craft which the Cabots and the Frobishers could not possibly have imagined: the atomic submarine. U.S.S. *Nautilus* did, without too much trouble, what the hard old-timers could not possibly do. The passage is in use today. The Arctic may yet be a highway rather than a barrier. Does not a faint touch of that lost sense of wonder return?

Maybe not, except for a very few. And yet the world may be on the verge of becoming, once again, what it always was until recently, a world of infinite possibilities and unimaginable horizons. We apparently stand today in respect to exploration about where Western man stood in 1490—on the edge of something that could restore the old sense of limitless vistas.

There is in the world now an international body of knowledge—imperfect, confused, possibly in the end impractical—which, without too great an effort, can be equated with the knowledge that existed nearly five centuries ago regarding the exploration of this globe: the knowledge of the road to outer space. There are the experts, who have learned a little more than the rest of us know—scientists who can be pulled away from their own countries to work for any nation that has the money, the determination, and the basic sense of insecurity to demand the enlisting of their services. (Much of the exploration of this earth was done by countries which feared that their neighbors had got the bulge on them.) Ventures are being made; the open sea, once again, seems to be a gateway to the undreamed-of, and the fact that this sea is the perilous void of interstellar space, instead of the equally perilous void of intercontinental salt water, makes very little difference.

The caravels are out, and nobody can be sure where they may eventually go. Instead of being at the end of a great era, it is just possible that we are approaching the beginning of an infinitely greater one. Any teenager addicted to science fiction can testify that the sense of wonder is being regained. Can we, really, be certain that a new upsurge of energy and a feeling of confidence will not some day come back with it?

N CHOOSING A SUBJECT

The biographer in between books is doubly vulnerable because biography seems to be everybody's business. For the novelist, the plot of his next book is a private matter between himself and his typewriter—a happy secrecy, permitting conception without interference of seduction or extracurricular rape. With me at least, my last work is no sooner on the stands than letters come, suggesting a subject. The grandmothers of strangers are crying from the grave, it seems, for literary recognition; it is bewildering, the number of salty grandfathers, aunts and uncles that languish unappreciated. Telegrams propose a day and hour of appointment, when I can have the privilege of learning the circumstances and (irresistible) character of the deceased. Sometimes the subject is not decently dead but signs the telegram, in which case wires must be dispatched, stating regret and my plans for immediate departure to far places. Subjects have been known to ring my doorbell, unannounced, and standing upon the mat, all in the open air begin what salesmen call their pitch.

Rival publishers send tactful letters. (How gratified one would have been to receive them, twenty years ago!) If my publisher has not already made the suggestion, their own list could profitably include a biography of George Washington, Jane Addams, Edna Millay, Justice Brandeis, John Marshall, Roger Taney, Clara Schumann or old Judge Sewall of Massachusetts who sentenced the witches and repented. My own publisher, however, is not sleeping. He telephones from Boston with two suggestions, which he refers to as "ideas." Two beauties, he says cheerfully. What is the matter, don't I even want to hear the names?

I do not, and it is best to say so. The fact is that suggested subjects can be dangerous for the biographer, especially if they are forced and pushed, with rewards offered. Some literary forms do not lend themselves to commission-writing; the product emerges tasting of the shop, like fruits laid on, a hothouse breed, lacking the tang and scent of the native product. It is my contention (and it is not original) that an author's books, no matter what his professed subject, are actually about the author. It does not follow that the product is egotistical; Boswell bore little likeness to Samuel Johnson. Yet, whatever form the writer chooses—fiction, poetry, biography—his books are written because he has something to discharge, some ghost within that struggles for release. In company with other writers, I am often asked if I am "with book," or when I expect to "give birth." There is reason for this tired witticism; in his book an author actually is discharging some part of himself. Could one imagine Carlyle's *French Revolution* being conceived, as subject, by anyone but the author—Froude's *History of the Reign of Queen Elizabeth*, Parkman's *Oregon Trail*, De Voto's *Across the Wide Missouri*? The very titles bear their author's stamp. Here, nothing is machine-made. It is all done by hand, as we used to say of good millinery; its very faults are the craftsman's and convey his message. These books proceed unevenly, like human beings, one moment prosy, the next moment dramatic. They are marked, in short, by that quality which beyond all qualities is difficult for the artist to achieve and impossible to counterfeit, the quality of life itself.

—Catherine Drinker Bowen, Adventures of a Biographer. *Little, Brown & Co. in association with the Atlantic Monthly Press. Copyright 1946, © 1958, 1959 by Catherine Drinker Bowen.*

N FINISHING A VERY LONG BOOK

It was on the day, or rather night, of the 27th of June, 1787, between the hours of eleven and twelve, that I wrote the last lines of the last page, in a summer house in my garden. After laying down my pen I took several turns in a berceau, or covered walk of acacias, which commands a prospect of the country, the lake and mountains. The air was temperate, the sky was serene, the silver orb of the moon was reflected from the waters, and all nature was silent. I will not dissemble the first emotions of joy on recovery of my freedom, and perhaps, the establishment of my fame. But my pride was soon humbled, and a sober melancholy was spread over my mind, by the idea that I had taken an everlasting leave of an old and agreeable companion, and that, whatsoever might be the future fate of my History, the life of the historian must be short and precarious.

—Edward Gibbon, Memoirs, *1796*

What Samuel Wrought

CONTINUED FROM PAGE 15

encouragement," Allston wrote to Jedidiah, "he will be a great painter."

In the end Morse did not meet with the encouragement he felt he deserved. When they summoned him from England he had written to his parents that to return meant to throw away "the talents which Heaven has given me for the higher branches of art." The cultural climate of America would drive him into being "a mere portrait painter." The great majority of the hundreds of paintings he produced in the next thirty years were indeed portraits. John Adams once declared he would not give a fig for a Raphael, but even he sat for Morse when the young artist returned from abroad.

Although he enjoyed prosperous seasons and painted prominent people, including President James Monroe as well as Adams, the financial returns were not consistently ample. When he took a wife and sired a family, he found it all but impossible to keep a roof over their heads. He was never a provident sort. In 1822, at a time when his wife and children were obliged to move in with the elder Morses, Finley impulsively made a donation of five hundred dollars to the Yale library. For him, money was never simply an end in itself. It stood for the recognition of merit, the successful accomplishment of a mission, the reward of virtue—and fame, perhaps, if that were the will of God.

The climate of our booming democracy was not actually so harsh for artists. A number of Morse's contemporaries enjoyed a very decent success with their landscapes and their genre pieces, not to mention their portraits. But Morse, guided by his own inner lights, set the terms on which he would accept recognition and admit success as an artist, and these his countrymen were not prepared to meet. In 1822 he completed the first of the only two large compositions he ever attempted, *Congress Hall* or *The Old House of Representatives*. With its eighty-odd miniature portraits, its solemn, dramatically lighted setting, and its skillful handling of perspective, the painting was a major accomplishment. But it was not a great imaginative vision such as he had dreamed of creating. It was a tour de force, a fine example of proficient reporting. By putting it on the road he hoped to match the success several of his fellow artists were enjoying with their large, traveling showpieces that "played" to big paying audiences. But when he unveiled his own attraction, the public seemed not to care. After a few trials, *Congress Hall* was rolled away for years, then sold for a mere thousand dollars and taken to England.

At one point in later life Morse expressed the wish that, except for a few he valued as family documents,

his pictures might all be destroyed. He felt he had failed as an artist, and, for a few generations at least, posterity concurred by remembering him almost exclusively as the internationally renowned inventor. But his invention has long since become a commonplace convenience, an almost rudimentary survival in an age that relays its communications from satellites hurtling through outer space, and today it is much easier to judge Morse fairly as an artist. Not only can we see his work without the personal prejudices that led him to condemn it and without the blinding distraction of his fame in other fields, we can see it more clearly against the total accomplishment of his time. And we can find among his paintings some that are as fine as any by his American contemporaries. Indeed, in their combination of technical competence and perceptive rendering, his portraits of Judge Mitchell, Benjamin Silliman, and William Cullen Bryant—to name a few—have rarely if ever been excelled by an artist in this country.

In what he did do, Morse was a very successful painter, except that in the long run he could not make a decent living by his brush. It was in what he did not do, did not try to do, but felt he should do, that he failed in his own eyes. For a long time before he was willing to concede any incongruity in his personal concept of the true nature of art, Morse labored with the hope of educating the world around him to higher standards of taste. He would lead his fellow artists in the promotion of their own interest, call public attention to the dignity of their calling, and thus, perhaps, serve his country as well as by exercising his own heaven-sent talent. For, as he wrote his wife shortly before her early death, he was determined to do "something for the Arts in our country."

With militant enthusiasm he helped form and, in 1826, assumed the presidency of the new National Academy of Design, an organization of working artists that would exhibit contemporary American art, offer instruction and awards, and set professional standards of excellence. As president, a position he continued to fill for the next nineteen years, Morse threw his greatest energies into Academy affairs. "Finley is well and in good spirits," wrote one of his brothers at the time, "though not advancing very rapidly in his business. He is full of the Academy and of his lectures—can hardly talk on any other subject. I despair of ever seeing him rich or even at ease in his pecuniary circumstances from efforts of his own, though able to do it with so little effort."

The activities of the new academy brought Morse into head-on collision with the earlier-established American Academy of Fine Arts, an organization controlled and patronized largely by public-spirited laymen, and its venerable president, Colonel John Trumbull. The principle that artists should and could operate in a union of professional interest in itself brought sharp criticism. Morse's first address as president was immediately challenged by a broadside printed in the *North American Review*. Referring to the rise of science and industry in America and the booming activity of metropolitan New York, the anonymous commentator observed: "We are not prepared to see the American system, as it is called, extended to literature or the arts. It would be the worst policy for the artists. Painting and sculpture are not among the necessaries of life. Much as they improve and adorn society, a taste for them is not even the necessary accompaniment of a high degree of civilization." And, in another blast: "We would not have the arts degraded even in favor of the artists . . . We can hardly hope that the masterpieces of ancient art are ever to be surpassed here or in Europe. The forms and occupations of society are growing every day less favorable to the highest efforts of the imagination. We live in an age of utility . . . In this cultivation of the reason, the imagination loses its power. Eloquence, poetry, painting, and sculpture, do not belong to such an age; they are already declining, and they must give way before the progress of popular education, science, and the useful arts. . . ." But these attacks only strengthened Morse's stubborn determination to lead his academy to the high destiny he envisioned for it. He fought for his cause relentlessly over the years until, at last, he felt he could confidently transfer the leadership to younger men.

But neither the frustrations he had met in his own art nor the early struggles of the academy had yet killed off the aspirations of Morse's youth. He still planned to return to Europe, to the continent, where he had never gone, "to rekindle my former ardor and renew my recollection of excellence in the art." And in 1829, buttressed by a number of private commissions for copies and originals to be made in Italy and France, he left on his grand tour. In those more enlightened parts of the world, he felt with fresh conviction, he would execute some painting worthy of his ideals, a picture that would indeed do "something for the Arts in our country." If all went well, it might also replenish his purse.

Morse's tour lasted almost three years. Those were turbulent times in Europe. He witnessed the uprisings in the Papal States and saw them put down with the aid of Metternich's Austrian troops. In Paris the radical movement, with Lafayette, patriarch of republican causes, at its head, had fizzled out after the July Revolution of 1830 when Louis Philippe was elevated to the throne. The liberal revolts in Poland were crushed, again with help from Metternich. Morse talked at length with Lafayette about the threats to human freedom from meddling autocracy and heard denunciations which he never forgot leveled at the far-reaching authority of the pope.

During most of the last spring and summer, in 1832, he worked himself almost to the point of exhaustion on what was to be a "great work"—his painting of a gallery in the Louvre, with thirty-odd selected masterpieces represented as though they were hanging together on the walls of the Salon Carré. Morse learned much from this intimate, workaday contact with the old masters. James Fenimore Cooper, who was so constantly at his side in the gallery that, as he said, his face was as familiar in the Louvre as any Van Dyck, assured Morse that his picture "must take" with the American public. And unwittingly most damning, he wrote home from Paris that Morse "copies admirably."

Somewhere along the line Morse's early ambition had lost its bearings. He was revealing the splendors of the past great ages of painting, as he had once said he would do; he was taking Titian, Raphael, Leonardo, and the other masters to the American people in the hope they might be willing to look at copies of works they would probably never see in the originals; but he was not shining with his own light. He was dealing in second-hand goods.

Morse left France on the ship *Sully* in the fall of 1832 with his Louvre painting ready for finishing at home and his mind brimming with the conversations he had held with old Lafayette. There was also another excitement on the eve of his departure. He had seen the semaphores in Paris announcing the suppression of the Poles; it distressed him additionally that the news had come so slowly, so late, and he was soon excited about the practical possibilities of transmitting intelligence by electricity.

Morse's idea of instantaneous communication was hardly a new one. More than eighty years earlier Benjamin Franklin had, among his other electrical experiments, fired spirits with a spark sent from the opposite side of the Schuylkill to entertain his friends. He was concerned that nothing more useful to mankind could be developed out of such a "magical" trick; but it was, in fact, a visual electrical semaphore of sorts. In 1753 an anonymous letter in the *Scots Magazine* had proposed sending alphabetized messages through insulated wires charged by batteries. Twenty-one years later a very primitive sort of electric telegraph had actually been operated in Geneva by Lesage; and over the decades that followed, every advance in the understanding of electricity had generated new proposals for "lightning" communication. Even while Morse was abroad, his compatriot Joseph Henry had rung bells from a distance—or, rather, over a mile-length of wire strung about a room—by means of his powerful "intensity" battery and electromagnet.

Others were attacking the question in similar and in different ways, but at the start Morse was largely unaware of the extent or the significance of their explorations. He approached the problem as if it were his alone to master. Although he was far from being abreast of the advanced studies that were paving the way from various directions, he was not altogether unprepared for this foray into applied science. At Yale, as a youngster, he had heard lectures on elec-

to my next.— I am still continuing my studies, at present I am preparing a picture for Somerset House exhibition; "Dorothea" from Don Quixote; I think I shall not be able to see my native country for some years yet to come; I must return a painter I obtained a prize of a gold me—

From London in the spring of 1814, Morse wrote friends in New York of his determination not to return home until he had become a painter.

tricity by Benjamin Silliman and Jeremiah Day and had witnessed their demonstrations. Before leaving for Europe he had attended the courses in electricity given at the New York Athenaeum by James Freeman Dana. That was enough, in any case, to feed his interest, and during the six weeks' crossing on the *Sully,* Morse quickly and brilliantly thrashed out in his imagination his own concept of a recording telegraph. He sketched out his ideas in a notebook, showing a single circuit of wire contrived to carry a coded message—essentially dots, dashes, and spaces—and a device for recording these intervals by electromagnetic action on a moving strip of paper. The scheme he outlined was pitifully far from being an actual working plan. It ignored, or rather did not envision, a maze of practical difficulties that would have to be faced. But however naïvely, it projected the principles of his ultimate invention with remarkable prescience.

When Morse disembarked from the *Sully* at New York in November, 1832, his mind was burning with his new project, but he returned to distractions that he could not—and some that he would not—avoid. He had come home to witness the great rising tide of Jackso-

nian democracy. Into this social ferment was being poured each year in increasing numbers, swarming shiploads of immigrants. They were being funneled into New York by the tens and hundreds of thousands. For Morse these alien hordes represented a menace to his native land. There would follow an inevitable leveling down from those ideals he felt so strongly must never be relaxed. It was a threat that neither education nor traditional religion could meet, he believed, since so many of the newcomers clung to the authority of the Roman Catholic Church.

As Emerson remarked, a national faith thrives best when its prophets have a fallacy to expose, a subversion to combat, an ogre to demolish. Over the years leading to mid-century, self-appointed guardians of democracy found in Catholicism the public enemy that called forth their gravest apprehensions. Morse was not offended by the religious practices of Catholics, as were so many of his rabid compatriots. But in this alien and autocratic organization he saw a plot, engineered from Europe in the manner of Metternich and the pope that prince had supported, to undermine the free institutions of his own beloved country. Years before Jedidiah Morse had preached vehement sermons against the Society of the Illuminati, supposedly a radical branch of Freemasonry, in whose separate oaths and secret ceremonies he saw the subversion of a free society. It raised an old and perplexing problem that has never been answered because it never can be: how free can a free society afford to be without endangering its freedom? Now Jedidiah's son found the same conspiratorial menace in Catholicism; Lafayette would have agreed with him. Morse joined the crusade to stem the tide.

In books and pamphlets, the painter-turned-politician cried out his warnings against the "conspiracy." His anxieties led him into the most hysterical forms of witch-hunting. The anti-Catholic press, exploiting a bonanza, put out lurid fictions of lust and murder in convents and monasteries. The best seller of all was Maria Monk's *Awful Disclosures . . . in the Hôtel Dieu Nunnery at Montreal,* a fairy tale littered with the most titillating obscenities. Maria ultimately died in prison, where she had been lodged after picking the pocket of a sister prostitute. But while her "revelations" were fresh, Morse accepted them with sympathy and fervor.

These were troubled years in Morse's life. He squandered precious energy in his defense of democracy as he treasured it. In 1836 he felt it was his bounden duty to run for mayor of New York on the ticket of the Native American Democratic Association. Fortunately for everyone, including himself, he received less than fifteen hundred votes. It was not the end of his political involvements, but it should have been.

During all this unhappy performance, Morse's circumstances grew ever more urgent. He had exhausted his resources on his grand tour, and he desperately needed money simply to exist without charity, let alone provide a home for his now motherless children, who had been left with relatives. The Louvre picture was his most immediate money-making project, and he must find time to finish it. Now, in spite of gnawing poverty, the excitements of Nativism, and his dreams of a telegraph, during the five years following his return from Europe this strange and often confusing man painted some of his most brilliant portraits. He was at the full maturity of his powers as an artist, yet his commissions were few. He was paid sixty dollars for the *Allegorical Landscape Showing New York University,* a telling indication of how uncertain his brush became when he departed from the facts before his eyes and trusted to his imagination. It is a confused picture, although it provides a welcome reminder of the "fine Gothick building" on the east side of Washington Square, in one of whose leaking and drafty tower rooms he had taken up his quarters. He had been appointed to the faculty to teach sculpture and painting in the newly formed University of the City of New York—the first professorship of fine arts in any American college, and a very meager source of income.

He also managed to finish his *Exhibition Gallery of the Louvre* and with high hopes put it up for public exhibition in August, 1833. Yet for all Cooper's predictions and some glowing effusions that appeared in the New York press, it was another dismal financial failure. Even that was not enough to kill his aspirations. The worst blow of all came four years later when, after a long period of intermittent great expectations, a very highly recommended proposal that he be commissioned to paint a historical scene for one of the four undecorated panels in the rotunda of the Capitol was flatly rejected by Congress. Yet, when his influential and wealthy friends rallied round after that humiliation and commissioned him to paint any historical scene he chose, for three thousand dollars, he never did get around to it. He had been seduced by a new mistress whose claims on his interests were irresistible. To the consternation of most of his respectful students and colleagues, he was everlastingly preoccupied with wires and batteries and magnets.

Some years later Morse observed that he had not abandoned art, but that art had abandoned him. Painting may have been a smiling mistress to many, he wrote his old friend Cooper, "but she has been a cruel jilt to me . . . my idea of that profession *was* perhaps too exalted; I may say *is* too exalted. I leave it to others, more worthy to fill the niches of art." If there is room for error in such matters, it might as well be said that Providence had miscast him as an artist. Or had he misunderstood the "call" that had come to him a quarter of a century earlier? Morse had spent a full half of his life before he put down his brushes. But in his canvases he had never realized the mood of magic that now filled his dreams of telegraphy. Actually, since his student days he had never tried to climb to "the higher branches of art," because no one offered him enough money to make it worth his while. He did, in fact, almost starve in a garret, but, unlike the starving genius of romance, he did not improve his time by creating masterpieces the world might one day come to recognize. He waited for the big commissions that would release his spirit, and they did not come; he suffered, but at length turned to other things.

For a while Morse continued to think of his invention as a way of making enough money to free himself at last for the full pursuit of his muse, without the crass consideration of commissions, as in youth he had thought of a fire-pump apparatus he had invented with his brother and, later, of an idea for a marble-cutting machine. But in the spring and summer of 1837 news from England reported that substantial advances were being made in telegraphy overseas. If he did not quickly stake a firm claim in the field, he would be beaten to the goal; everything he had done so far would be wasted and his hopes gone.

In Morse's new role the most obdurate circumstances were not enough to thwart his purpose. The need to work fast converted his interest into an obsession, and out of this emerged a new sense of exaltation that he needed to satisfy his own soul. "God knows me better than I know myself . . . ," he wrote one of his brothers. "I shall therefore be sustained in all events."

Sustained or not, he was off to a late start. Morse was almost blissfully unaware of his own ignorance. He lacked adequate scientific knowledge; he seems not to have known of Henry's crucial experiments. He lacked the mechanical skill to make his own materials with any professional finesse. He lacked money to promote his scheme. And, in general, he faced a chilling skepticism in the world about him. His friends spoke sadly of the "miserable delusion" that had seized this warmly admired teacher and artist. If not at the start, however, Morse in the end got the help he needed from many sources, so many that he was never sure just where it had come from. Sometimes in stubborn pride he refused to concede that some of the most constructive suggestions were anything but his own earlier discoveries.

At the beginning, a university colleague, Professor Leonard Gale, called Morse's attention to Henry's studies and publications; and from that point on Henry himself gave Morse generous encouragement and indispensable advice, including the idea for the relays which would renew and sustain faint signals over many miles of wire. Before this priceless tip, the impulse was too feeble to travel any important distance. In September, 1837, now working with the intensity battery Henry had demonstrated years ago, Morse succeeded in sending a message through seventeen hundred feet of wire that he had strung about one of the university rooms. His recording apparatus had been assembled out of oddments that came to hand—the works of dismantled clocks, an old table, a stretcher from one of the canvases he would never paint—but the success of that crude contrivance brought Morse the financial aid and the skilled mechanical help he had to have to carry on. Stephen Vail, prosperous owner of the Speedwell Iron Works in New Jersey, offered to manufacture a more refined and practical version of Morse's device that could be shown to "the powers that be" in Washington. Vail's son Alfred, an accomplished mechanic in his own right, entered a formal partnership with Gale and Morse that same month. According to its terms, any contributions to the success of their enterprise would be credited to and patented in Morse's name as inventor, an agreement that ultimately obscured the magnitude of the constructive advice and practical service Alfred Vail gave to the project.

When the improved instrument was shown in Washington early in 1838, it evoked excited interest but won no tangible support. The demonstration did, however, add a fourth partner to Morse's group—Francis Ormond Jonathan Smith, "Fog" Smith, who as chairman of the House Committee on Commerce, sublimely indifferent to any conflict of interest in promoting the cause of the partnership in government circles, asked Congress for an appropriation of thirty thousand dollars. With Smith as companion, Morse went abroad to secure foreign patent protection for his invention there, pending more promising developments in America. He returned home in a few months empty-handed (and without having gone near the Louvre). Europe was developing its own plans for telegraphy—some were already in action—and Morse's proposals were rejected.

Morse had to wait six more years for the success he felt must be his, six lean years during which his discouraged partners drifted away from their common objective, and Morse himself at times went hungry. But his determination was now fixed and inflexible. He continued to seek and get the advice of Henry; he went on tinkering, sending submarine messages from the Battery in New York to Governor's Island (and prophesying the Atlantic cable)—and waiting doggedly for Congress to act.

He was still president of the National Academy, but he did not turn to painting to provide for his wants. What he did resort to was another new invention, daguerreotypy. He had met Daguerre on his last visit to Paris, had admired the new method of "drawing" invented by the French artist, and had enthusiastically and successfully proposed him as an honorary member of the National Academy. Here was a device, Morse pointed out to the academicians, that would put an end to the "sketchy, slovenly daubs" of artists who had neither the intelligence nor the skill to master details in their renderings; here, indeed, was "Rembrandt perfected."

Such remarks sparked an immediate controversy, of course, and one that was long in subsiding, if indeed it ever has. If you listened to that sort of theory, Thomas Cole wrote a friend in 1840, "you would be led to suppose that the poor craft of painting was knocked in the head by this new machinery for making Nature take her own likeness, and we [artists] nothing to do but give up the ghost . . . the art of painting is creative, as well as an imitative art, and is in no danger of being superseded by any mechanical contrivance." The irony is inescapable; Morse himself had given up the ghost concerning what he had once considered the inspired image. There was no turning back.

His efforts in daguerreotypy were successful enough, but they involved him in still another controversy. Charges of plagiarism, claims of prior developments, and other difficulties with competitors and counterclaimants arose. As a financial venture his career with a camera was a failure, but Morse is still referred to with respect as the father of American photography.

In the spring of 1843 a bid to finance a test line of telegraph started on its tortuous way through Congress. All but abandoned by his partners, though still heartily supported by Henry, Morse had continued to press his interests in Washington and in December had demonstrated his improved equipment. The bid was subjected to disparaging jokes and even crude ridicule on the floor of Congress. Morse was ready to give up all hope, pack his bags, and return to New York; he had just enough money to get there. But by what seemed almost a greater miracle than the telegraph itself, at a late hour of the last day of its session, Congress appropriated the thirty thousand dollars that Fog Smith had asked for in 1838.

The test line was to run forty-one miles between Baltimore and Washington. Smith awarded himself the contract for the construction, and Morse borrowed fifty dollars from a former pupil to buy a new hat and a new pair of pants. The partnership suddenly came to life again, and work was started.

The following months were a continuous nightmare for Morse. Letting the contracts and commandeering the materials proved complicated enough; but then the partners turned to squabbling, and, to cap the climax, when twenty-three thousand dollars of the appropriation had been exhausted on only a small part of the underground route and time was running out, Smith's existing lines were found to be shoddy and defective. The job had to be redone with what money was left, and quickly. Morse felt he was on the brink of total disgrace. This was in February, 1844. He flew to Henry for advice and, reassured, returned to the task with redoubled determination. But without the major effort of Ezra Cornell, who had been appointed construction engineer and strung a much cheaper and faster line on poles, the whole project would have failed. By May, however, the work was done. On the twenty-fourth of that month, in a chamber of the Supreme Court in the Capitol, Morse dispatched the well-remembered message that formally demonstrated his accomplishment before the world: "What hath God wrought!" *

Whether Morse ever read Thoreau's remarks or not, at the time they were written he might not have disagreed violently with them. He hoped to reserve this instrument that God had wrought through him only for communications of urgent importance; he felt it should not be used as a mere convenience. He feared the abuse of power by selfish men if his lightning communications were not controlled for the common good. He asked the government to assume jurisdiction.

Virtue, in this case, was not its own reward alone, for Morse's partnership quickly mushroomed into a vast commercial enterprise. Both the telegraph and his own finances were soon entrusted to more competent advisers, so that the improvident Finley at last made his fortune. But the sunset of the story is no more purely golden than its noon, and, as before,

* That event was an anticlimax of sorts. Morse had already used the wires as work progressed to report to Washington on the Whig and Democratic conventions in Baltimore.

MEMORIAL SERVICES
IN HONOR OF THE LATE
SAMUEL F. B. MORSE,
IN THE
HALL OF THE HOUSE OF REPRESENTATIVES,
April 16, 1872, at half-past 7 o'clock.

This ticket admits one lady to the GALLERY reserved for ladies only, and is positively not transferable.

No 39

NEW-YORK HISTORICAL SOCIETY

On April 16, 1872, two weeks after Morse died, the Hall of Representatives was thronged for formal memorial services attended by President Grant and the Cabinet, the Justices of the Supreme Court, governors of the states, and members of both houses of Congress. The Marine band played, and Speaker James G. Blaine read a message from the telegraph operators of Britain, paying their respects to the inventor.

many of the clouds were self-made. As the acknowledged inventor, Morse for years to come still had to protect the validity of his patents against the shrewdest and sharpest attacks. It was even more difficult to protect his reputation against the claims of those whose help in the past he now tended to dispute or ignore. These were not his most glorious moments. When the Civil War came, and his telegraph played a vital part in it, the aging Nativist seemed mainly preoccupied with his hatred for Lincoln. He agreed with those who thought slavery "divinely ordained," and, if Lincoln were re-elected in 1864, he announced, Samuel F. B. Morse would leave the country.

Like so many pledges of the kind, this one was never carried out. Finley stayed. The reputation survived, for the great achievement cast its long, protective shadow over the errors. Even so fervent an abolitionist as the poet Bryant did not turn against him or fail, as we have seen, to do the old man honor. And the first formal words over the telegraph linger on through history, the unforgettable reminder not only of the mission accomplished but of the Puritan fulfilled. Providence at last had found him a worthy agent for its purposes.

Marshall B. Davidson, author of Life in America, *is a frequent contributor to* AMERICAN HERITAGE. *His most recent article was* "Penn's City: American Athens" *in the February, 1961, issue.*

For further reading: Samuel F. B. Morse and American Democratic Art, *by Oliver W. Larkin (Little, Brown, 1954);* The American Leonardo, A Life of Samuel F. B. Morse, *by Carleton Mabee (Knopf, 1943).*

"There is room for all, and millions more"

America is a wonderful country, endowed by the Omnipotent with natural advantages which no other can boast of; and the mind can hardly calculate upon the degree of perfection and power to which, whether the States are eventually separated or not, it may in the course of two centuries arrive. At present all is energy and enterprise; every thing is in a state of transition, but of rapid improvement—so rapid, indeed, that those who would describe America now would have to correct all in the short space of ten years; for ten years in America is almost equal to a century in the old continent. Now, you may pass through a wild forest, where the elk browses and the panther howls. In ten years, that very forest, with its denizens, will, most likely, have disappeared, and in their place you will find towns with thousands of inhabitants; with arts, manufactures, and machinery, all in full activity.

In reviewing America, we must look upon it as showing the development of the English character under a new aspect, arising from a new state of things. If I were to draw a comparison between the English and the Americans, I should say that there is almost as much difference between the two nations at this present time, as there has long been between the English and the Dutch. The latter are considered by us as phlegmatic and slow; and we may be considered the same, compared with our energetic descendants. Time to an American is everything and space he attempts to reduce to a mere nothing. By the steam-boats, rail-roads, and the wonderful facilities of water-carriage, a journey of five hundred miles is as little considered in America, as would be here a journey from London to Brighton. *"Go ahead"* is the real motto of the country; and every man does push on, to gain in advance of his neighbour. The American lives twice as long as others; for he does twice the work during the time that he lives. He begins life sooner: at fifteen he is considered a man, plunges into the stream of enterprize, floats and struggles with his fellows. In every trifle an American shows the value he puts upon time. He rises early, eats his meals with the rapidity of a wolf, and is the whole day at his business. If he be a merchant, his money, whatever it may amount to, is seldom invested; it is all floating—his accumulations remain active; and when he dies, his wealth has to be collected from the four quarters of the globe.

Now, all this energy and activity is of English origin; and were England expanded into America, the same results would be produced. To a certain degree, the English were in former times what the Americans are now; and this it is which has raised our country so high in the scale of nations; but since we have become so closely packed—so crowded, that there is hardly room for the population, our activity has been proportionably cramped and subdued. But, in this vast and favoured country, the very associations and impressions of childhood foster and ripen the intellect, and precociously rouse the energies. The wide expanse of territory already occupied—the vast and magnificent rivers—the boundless regions, yet remaining to be peopled—the rapidity of communication—the dispatch with which every thing is effected, are evident almost to the child. To those who have rivers many thousand miles in length, the passage across the Atlantic (of 3,500 miles) appears but a trifle; and the American ladies talk of spending the winter at Paris with as much indifference as one of our landed proprietors would, of going up to London for the season.

We must always bear in mind the peculiar and wonderful advantages of *country,* when we examine America and its form of government; for the country has had more to do with upholding this democracy than people might at first imagine. Among the advantages of democracy, the greatest is, perhaps, that *all start fair:* and the boy who holds the traveller's horse, as Van Buren is said to have done, may become the president of the United States.

But it is the *country,* and not the government, which has been productive of such rapid strides as have been made by America. Indeed, it is a query whether the form of government would have existed down to this day, had it not been for the advantages derived from the vast extent and boundless resources of the territory in which it was established. Let the American direct his career to any goal he pleases, his energies are unshackled; and, in the race, the best man must win. There is room for all, and millions more.

From Captain Frederick Marryat's Diary in America *(1839), edited by Jules Zanger and published by the University of Indiana Press.*